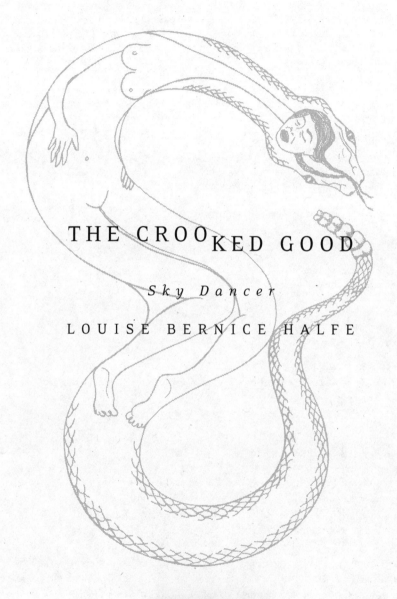

THE CROOKED GOOD

Sky Dancer

LOUISE BERNICE HALFE

COTEAU BOOKS

Edited by Séan Virgo
Cree language material edited by Jean Okimâsis, miywâsin ink
Book and cover design by Duncan Campbell
Cover and interior images: "Snake Woman," by Paul Lapointe

Printed and bound in Canada at Gauvin Press

Library and Archives Canada Cataloguing in Publication

Halfe, Louise Bernice, 1953-
The crooked good / Louise Bernice Halfe.

Poems.
Includes some text in Cree.
ISBN 978-1-55050-372-2

1. Cree Indians—Poetry. I. Title.
PS8565.A4335C76 2007   C811'.54   C2007-905493-5

POD October 2011

2517 Victoria Avenue
Regina, Saskatchewan
Canada S4P 0T2
www.coteaubooks.com

Available in Canada from:
Publishers Group Canada
2440 Viking Way
Richmond, British Columbia
Canada V6V 1N2

Coteau Books gratefully acknowledges the financial support of its publishing program by: the Saskatchewan Arts Board, the Canada Council for the Arts, the Government of Canada through the Canada Book Fund, the Government of Saskatchewan through the Creative Economy Entrepreneurial Fund and the City of Regina Arts Commission.

A thousand half-loves must be forsaken
to take one whole heart home.

*– Rumi: The Book of Love: poems of ecstasy & longing
(Translation by Coleman Barks)*

Everyone is trying to finish things right away, then when he falls short at times to make it look a certain way, to make it look nice, he cannot do it; he doesn't control his actions properly, he can't think for himself properly and his feelings are not right, his heart is not in the right place, he is unable to appreciate anything. Perhaps that is the reason why man is having a difficult time. And man is also creating his own illness. Perhaps it is the result of our not praying properly, that we don't understand our Father although each day we look at his creation. We don't recognize what he does, perhaps that is why we continue to miss things here and there.

– J.P. CARDINAL
Excerpt from Elder Cardinal's counselling words.

(Translated by Jean Okimâsis and Arok Wolvengrey)

CONTENTS

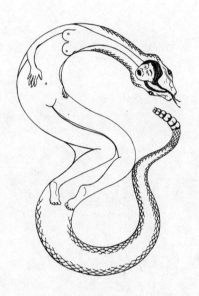

The End and the Beginning

I made a trip across the largest lake
I've ever seen
to where the long noses live.
There on the hill
Boulders sat
in a Talking Circle.
I walked around and gave tobacco.
They squeezed their stone-ground hands
on my chest
as I choked to a decision I had made.
My Beloved held me.
Though I never spoke of it,
somewhere in his secret lair he knew.

I've sat with Rib Woman
since *âtayôhkan* became Big Thunder
and her Big Heavens awoke in us.
Many of us have. Some of us never understand.
Some of us have learned to:
Incubate,
hatch these million eyes, these million
ears, these million noses, these ancient roots
that stem through our bodies.
It is these sun-runners who go deep in the
Dwelling.
Perhaps, I am one of them.

wêpinâson

Two women stare at each other.
Grunts, groans, rippling, meowing and cawing,
they spin these songs:
Of a brook searching. A crane meditating
A frog croaking. A mantis sucking on a fly.
A beaver caught in an iron jaw.
Thunder shuddered. A pair of lovers parted under a tree.
Lightning smiled through one's heart.
Dew rolled into the woman's basket.

The Inuit voices bounced, echoed against
their lodge, wet with death.

A deer rubbed her nose into her mate,
pranced into the meadow,
fell as an arrow flew.
Her robe sliced with fluttering hands.
Her bones become the scraper, skinning knife, needles
and flute. Her sinew thread, rawhide bowls, folding boxes,
drums and medicine bags.
Her skin a lodge of sticks and hide. Her hair, a mattress.
Close by, fur-covered men sat drumming.
This I saw, *ê-kwêskît* – Turn Around Woman. I am she.

ê-kwêskît - TURN-AROUND WOMAN

When I was growing up in the bush, on the hillside,
I watched the sun arrive from the dark, watched her slip
into the dark. I travelled. I didn't know the world back then.
I just travelled. I was afraid
I would never return. I tumbled that hillside
back into myself.

You can tell me
after you hear this story
if my name suits me.
I've yet to figure it out.

In Rib Woman
stories are born.
The Old Man called it psychology. Me,
I just dream it.

> *These gifted mysterious people of long ago,*
> kayâs kî-mamâhtâwisiwak iyiniwak,

my mother, Gone-For-Good, would say.

> *They never died. They are scattered here, there,*
> *everywhere, somewhere. They know the language,*
> *the sleep, the dream, the laws, these singers, these healers,*
> âtayôhkanak, *these ancient story keepers*

I, Turn-Around, am not one of them.

I was taught by Old people.
An Indian Man, a White Man.
An Indian Woman, a White Woman.
They worked in lairs, in the full veins of
Rib Woman.

I sat in their thicket, wailing.
The old ones navigated through my dreams.
Sometimes they dragged, scolded, cajoled,
cheered and celebrated.
I wanted to be with them. Like them.

I am not a saint. I am a crooked good.
My cousins said I was easy, therefore
I've never been a maiden.
I am seventy, but still
I carry my sins. Brothers-in-law
I meet for the first time wipe their hands
as if I am still among the maggots. I didn't
know their women wept when their men
slept in my bed. I am not a saint.

I married Abel, a wide green-eyed man. Fifty years now.
Inside Rib Woman I shook hands with promise.
Promise never forgot, trailed me year after year.
His Big Heavens a morning lake
drowns me in my lair.
I learned how to build Rib Woman
one willow at a time, one skin at a time.
I am only half done. This is part of the story.

I, *ê-kwêskît,* am a dreamer.
I dream awake. Asleep. On paper.
The Old Man said the universe,
the day, was the story. So,
every day I am born.
The Old White Man taught me
to unfold night visits.
The Old Woman taught me
all of it was real.
The Old White Woman helped me
To cry with the thunder.

Everyday is a Story

Outside my window stands a rust-orange needled tree.
Beneath it is a pine, branches with thick spikes.
They stand aloof. Sure-footed. On my bed lie three binders,
bellies ink-filled. They wait. My stomach talks. I am hungry
for voice, though I live in terror. Unsure what shape will arrive.
Voices in thought. A wish. A desire. A dream. A vision.
Fingers cannot catch their passing. Invisible Little People.
I am deaf though my ear strains. Perhaps it is a crazed beast
that buys a two-bit Stetson at a garage sale. But
it's just mother *aspin*, Gone-For-Good, though she is
anything but gone.

    aspin wears tams, a kerchief now and then, a loose sweater,
a v-neck dress whose waist is directly below her breasts. She sews
her dresses, same shape if fat layers or hunger arrives.
      Garters hold up
thick stockings, or cut-off ribbed socks at her ankles, and
moccasin rubbers. Her money stashed in small purses,
      she says she
is always broke. Then flashes her bank book.
Gone-For-Good buys our strawberries, lures us with money
and spits it out to watch the dog fight.
But I, *ê-kwêskît*, am ahead of my story.

I am inhaling mountains.
Voices skate, flow beneath ice shelves, grope through cracks
to catch each breath, freeze the voice to itself. A duck
splayed in ice still flying, its voice racing beneath slivers.
Voices from nose-blowing ravens, they grind sputum
beneath their heels, curious beady heavens crane, peer.

Female voices. Male. My husband's voice winds,
wraps around my body. Deeply patient, fevered, his slender
mouth an "O" of wet kisses. His voice a prayer lifting off a lake,
broad as a tree trunk, moves as an infant's finger.
He is woodsmoke, grassfire soot, grapefruit,
a writing paper, a song in the sweat lodge. A stake
in Rib Woman.

I build this story like my lair. One willow,
a rib at a time. Bent it into my hip, grounded into earth.
I walked the forest, hitchhiking seeds clung to my socks,
hopped into my pant cuff, bedded into the swollen lips
of my boots.
I walked slow, held a bucksaw, an axe.
Bled the willows, draped skins, hide, blankets, tarps
over their crippled bodies – this book took shape.
In this lair I lived in darkness. Dug a pit, heated
the grandfathers, till they sweated. Dreams dripped
from my breasts, from my many lips.

Have I told you where I grew up?
On a knoll, in a clearing. A small reserve called
wîhtikow sâkahikan, there they burned the flesh eater on ice.
That is another story.
We were divided by a creek, many hills,
cabins ruled by men. *aspin* and the rest
of the wives. Kept women. Even *nôhkomak*.
We competed with one another.
Stole. Shunned one another. Everyday events.
We were all saints.

aspin, Gone-For-Good, the cream-butter belly, the fat eater
lived when travel was horse and wagon.
     She stayed in the Ukranian
farmer's granary until *wâpistikwân* built her a log cabin.
They owned a pickup. She never learned to drive.
     They drove to
manawânis – where cowboys and Indians gathered,
     to town, to residential school to visit us.
     They stooked, picked rocks and roots.
     Shovelled manure,
worked in sugar beet fields. Janitored in sick buildings.
     They drifted.
Woods. Mountains. Back to *wîhtikow sâkahikan*.

Three-Person, Mechanic, *ospwâkan*, I, *ê-kwêskît*, *wâpan*,
we inherited laughter, mule skulls, working hands. None
escaped *pâhkahkos*. We travelled on brooms,
jalopies, luxury cars, airplanes, trains, ships.
We covered great distances. We all had loves. Secret loves.
Snake-tongued lovers. *aspin* believed in medicines.
Three-Person and Mechanic were like her. My medicine
came from the Old Men, the Old Women, I have no roots,
no herbs. Just
Dreams.

No one expected us, the brown-skins, to get anywhere.
Especially us women.

"*All their actions (my savages) are dictated
to them directly by the devil,
who speaks to them,
now in the form of a crow
or some similar bird,
now in the form of a flame
or a ghost,
and all this in dreams.
They consider the dream
as master of their lives,
It is the God of the country.
It is this which dictates them their feasts,
Their hunting,
Their fishing,
Their war,
Their trade with the French,
Their remedies,
Their dances,
Their games,
Their songs,*
[their loves]
*to cure a sick person,
they summon the sorcerer,
who without acquainting himself
with the disease of the patient,
sings,
and shakes his tortoise shell;
he gazes into the water
and sometimes into the fire,
to discover the nature of the disease.*"

"They believe in the immortality
of the soul,
which they believe to be corporeal
...they make no mention either of punishment
or reward
in the places which souls go after death.
And so they do not make any distinction
between the good and the bad,
the virtuous and the vicious;
And they honour equally the interment of both." [1]

And so *aspin* Gone-For-Good, Three Person,
Mechanic, *wâpan* and I, *ê-kwêskît*, lived...
Shared a story...
Sang into the dark.

First Sound

Hoooooooooooo. Ommmmmmmmmmm.
I listened to my breath,
dragged the sound
deep from my belly. Held it. Hooooooooooooooooooo.

When Rolling Head surfaced, she lunged,
let out a huge Ommmmmmmmmmmmmmmmmmmmmmmmmmm.
I thought of the man in a wheelchair,
mauve crocus on the side of his head. Ommmmm...
Ommmmmmmmmm. Ommmmmmmmmmmmm.
He filled the whole mall. Ommmmmmmmmmmm.
Beloved's sweet Ommmmmmmmmmmmmmmm
The echo of my breath Ommmmmmmmmmmmmmmm
Ommmmmmmm...are you making fun of me?
        He asked...mmmmmmmmmmmmm
Hooooooooooooooooo I'm having moooooooooooooooooooooooo
my own............Ommmmmmmmmmmmmmmmmm, as we came.

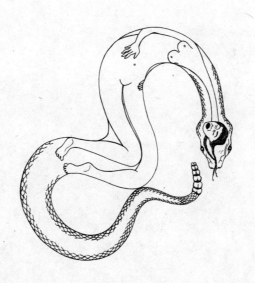

kayâs, long ago *aspin*, Gone-For-Good, fell through the ice,
where *wîhtikow* burned. Before that,
nôhkom threaded her mouth, boarding school pinned her arms,
then *wâpistikwân*, White Hair, snared her with cigarettes and
bootlegger's wine, big fist. *nôhkom* and *nimosôm* caged her
as if she was like Rapunzel. Then it was the pills.
We followed the wagon ruts.
Squatting against the wheel she mutters,

> *I sat many times in that hill and cried. Bruised so bad*
> *my belly hurt.*

wâpistikwân, White Hair, my handsome father,
fed fawns, captured owlets, dropped peanuts for pigeons and
squirrels at Stanley Park. He wrung the necks of geese,
roasted them and fed his skid-row friends.
He held me, *ê-kwêskît*, as if the plainness of my face
brought sunshine.
Still,
kittens shrieked their broken necks
slammed onto the earthen floor.

> *She wrote long love letters; fell to the ground when I left,*

he said as if the story was an everyday talk.

> *I did the leaving. I never marry him, White Hair*
> *did the marrying,*

aspin said. She moved
to Worm Heart City, worked as a janitor
in that sick building.
aspin, our mother, doesn't know how we lived in their sins.

Three Person, my big sister, Mechanic, *ospwâkan*,
my brothers, and *wâpan*, our little sister.
A family that slipped into each other's skins. A gift
that came to us from our ancestors.

Rolling Head wove her magic in those
thick winter nights, followed our family
from the tent to the frosted glass,
bled into the city heat,
scorched and branded our memory.

Three Person married *mâtahikan*. He was a caveman
        that danced like Karen Kain,
dragged Three Person, scraped and gouged her skull, left
white islands hidden beneath her hair. He
gave her fifteen hundred chants and hymns. She
begged at the foot of Mary,
starved at the foothills of Grandfather Stone.

Three Person clawed when she petted you.
Still,
giggle dropped out of her eyes now and then.
Giggle held her sides and rolled all over the floor
when she told me this story.

> *I was breastfeeding in a public area, minding my own business.*
> *When a white lady asked me to go to the lavatory.*
> *I didn't know what lavatory meant.*
> *When she told me,*
> *I looked at her and told her,*
> *"Tonight go eat your supper in the shit-house."*

Three Person was like that,
a cowboy Indian, a rising and storm-filled sun.
Not many people crossed her.

Mechanic left, made his living in *wîhtikow*'s belly.
For centuries his little man stole from boys, girls.
He borrowed a liver that loved coffee.
Someone else lent him a heart.
He injected his tired veins.

>   *People like you will eat grass when the hard times come,*

he prophesied.

I, *ê-kwêskît,* spoke to his new heart. He knew only the mantra
of my childhood name. Mechanic left his cubs
ready for skinning. I knew them as saplings. They've never
come to our door. And I
never look. I will not carry stained fingers,
hold injected veins.

ospwâkan is another noose on the whiteman's ledger.
White Hair once held a blade against his neck.
ospwâkan loved to laugh,

>   *I'll beat you till you have four legs.*

I see him still, a midget shaking his fist
against the bars.

wâpan was kindness. I, *ê-kwêskît,* watched
her crawl forward with her hand. Now, we are old.
Her hands are gnarled.
They cling to my skirt as if I am her mother.

I, *ê-kwêskît,* and *wâpan* shuddered beneath our bed.
Listened. Saw and listened. Three Person, Mechanic,
ospwâkan gone. Still we witnessed and heard.
We are mites on one another's skins. Nothing more.

I travelled with Gone-For-Good
on this disappeared road.

I wanted to see through her Big Heavens,
dig through *okiskêyihtamowin* – her knowledge
sad and lonely,
more than her bitter medicine.

Sugar-shack

Father, *wâpistikwân*, White Hair
was a tall muscular man.
Thick hair shingled elephant ears.
His calloused hands laid the sod roof
over the aspen frame of our cabin.
He poured water we hauled,
over dry grass we gathered, to mix
in clay. We squished mud between our toes,
slapped one another, otters dripping,
chinking the tear-stained walls.

The ashes have long been swallowed,
a gaping cellar covered. In memory
I walk the road where the cabin lived.
The last time I was there the windows were slatted,
sunlight streaked filtered walls, the door jammed.
In the vandalized room I collected *cîpayak*, wood,
fire smoke, grease, jelly rolls, dried meat.
Lifted my family off the earthen floor.

In dreams the cabin is half-finished, sun-filled
trees grow through the floor, their slender necks
climbing, their throats broad in the spacious rooms,
taper down as they push through the fallen roof.
The cabin weeps, leans on one dilapidated wall.
I wander room to room, the attic, cellar.
But there are no rooms.

I collect dresses: different sizes, shapes, colour.
Fill my bags. I am held in the arms of a loved one
long dead. They offer me wings born of fire.
Sit me at earth altars, feed me, sing me into a sorrowful sleep.

At dawn in the warmth of my office
I attempt to breathe this straw, give pine form, a
shape to thought. Too often I think it will not
materialize.

I am his child.
In wonder I remember what *wâpistikwân* built.

BRAIDS

cihcipistikwân, Rolling Head – *âtayôhkêwin.*
This legend nestles in the strawberry
where the nose sniffs and claws
root. Chokecherries scratch,
thicken the throat. Nothing can
suck out the fester, the clash of thunder and lightning
in Rib Woman and you, alone.
This is the beginning.

Rosehips boiled in honey
are not enough.
Skunk oil in lungs
is not enough.
Snake dripped in ears
is not enough.
Sweltering rocks split the acorn of
miskîsikwa – One's Big Heavens
making the clouds weep –
this is the beginning.

cihcipistikwân, she is
oil and water in dreams.

* *

cihcipistikwân stretches through her watery sleep.
Phantom arms. Feels. Squeezes, shuffles phantom toes.
Moves a foot. Through a membrane, a slight split in the
water, stretches her skin. Crawls through blubber.
Parts the belly of her eye. Centuries of waiting.
Where does the gathering of self begin?
What form?

She swam the thousand faces of her god.
âtayôhkan says when she drowned
she became a sturgeon. I don't know this.
I witness only what my ears held.

* *

Over brooks, ponds, rivers, lakes and seas,
her winds caused great floods. She cleared
her throat, swelled, tore dirt, shot arrow-spiked rains.
She sent flying flames, blistering fires.
She'd glide over mountains, unbuckle her soul,
colour the sky with her laughter, her howl.
She slept so long. Rocks are her spine, rivers
bury her seeds. No one knows her age. In the spring
Rolling Head awakens, becomes Rib Woman.
The lodge, her hair.
Willow people form her flesh, a basket woven
over weeping dreamers. The spring berry is her heart.
I told you this.
This dreamer. A ghost-faced woman with short blunt
black hair. Snakes dance on her shoulders, hips, belly
and thighs.
She dances between and under the arms
of the birch, spruce, aspen and pine.
Sometimes
the weeping dreamers awake
to her warmth
or they are dragged into her nightmare.
This, they share.
Her skin is a scar-wart face.
Still,

she chews stems, burrs cling
in loose hair, she spits.
The swan's breast
is filled with adulterous tales,
still
the obsessed continue
long after they first notice her.

* *

cihcipistikwân knows how yearning
crawls underground, blind hands
feeling in the lair. Desire flicks its tongue.
Rolling Head's Beloved woven in the starless night.
Her wail so loud
no one ever hears. Except him.

Her emerald lover
wrapped around her ankle
crushed her midriff, laid a reptilian head
on her hollow neck, gave her babies
against a log.

Her husband hunted,
deer and bear swung from broad shoulders,
happy with his bride,
asleep from her dreams.

Hush, oh hush, husband dear, it has nothing.
Nothing to do with you.

Listen: To the Story

We lived in tents, teepees before the four walls,
before the ugly, broken years.
Ears witnessed this story my mother, *aspin*,
unfurled.

aspin sat on a feathered buckskin blanket,
fingers bent willows. She dipped in the pail for red-stained
roots, her voice rising, falling, smoke curled toward the teepee's arms.
Fire crackled in front of her.

> kayâs êsa...*Long, long ago our people were filled with mystery
> and unexplainable powers*...ê-kî-mamâhtâwisicik.

We listened, skewered.
Waited long for this night.
Waited for the river to wear her ice-suet clothes.
Waited to wear our snowshoes, and track rabbits.
Waited. Waited.

The story gnawed, teased our infinite heavens.
The strawberry veins wrapped and nestled our hearts,
this Rolling Head. *cihcipistikwân.*

> kayâs êsa. *A man and a woman left the main camp
> with their two boys. They travelled, travelled, travelled,
> thick into the forest, thighs sucked in muskeg.
> The family fed the mosquitos.
> They gathered blue and cranberries, pin and bunch berries,
> mushrooms, rosehips, mint and muskeg.
> Juncos, chickadees, nuthatches, and whisky-jacks flew, scolding.
> Squirrels hoarded pine cones and hazelnuts. In the thicket
> bear, moose, elk and deer watched. The family
> pitched their skin tent upon a promise*

of birch and aspen syrup, spruce needle chews. A creek
sang itself into a gorged lake. Here shadows waved.

sâkâstêw *peeled the night cloud, stretched into daylight.*
The man gathered his hunting tools, bannock and rabbit.
He was gone all day.
pahkisimotâhk *curled into the darkness*
and pulled up her night blanket.
The man returned.
Supper unmade. Wood untouched. His wife's
tanning undone.

aspin took a swig of tea,
poked the embers, studied her basket.
Our moccasins slipped into our ears.
We sat. Tongues possessed. We learned how to feed
the sky dancers *wiyin*, fat,
in the owl dance of their death.
Drums and songs beckon them to rise
and give them form.

aspin crumbles a tobacco leaf, lifts it,
feeds the fire. Her voice guttural,
wind silent, flames creep, fix the air with small stares.

> *The man asked the boys what they did all day.*
> *The thoughts wrestled, twisted out: "Mother feeds us*
> *and scolds never to follow her, she gives us work."*
> *Mouths pointed to the forest.*

> *For days the father shadowed his wife's movements. One day*
> *she sat on a large log. Sang. Fist drummed.*

A snake slithered out
followed by small snakes, excited tails flipping,
squirmed under her warm hands. This he watched.
Hard.

He filled his bundle; tobacco, stone axe, arrows and bow.
Gave his sons an awl, a flint, a rock, a beaver's tooth.
Told his sons the medicine's secrets
 to be used only when the sky was red.

One day the man rose before the sun,
he drummed the log. The man bellowed.
His axe sliced the heads off each snake.
At camp, his wife still asleep,
he boiled broth, offered her the soup.
Her lips smacked thankful for the food.

Our bellies became a storm of worms.
We scratched our skulls, hair strands fell into our infinite heavens.
aspin's voice a drumstick against our ears,
stopped as we struggled to untangle her net.
She drank tea, gulping slowly, pushed
sweet grass into the embers. The wind
settled in her chest.

The woman shrieked, her lover trickling down her mouth.
The sky bled, the husband severed her head, and
cast her body to the heavens and he too ascends,
his body the milky way. Her body dressed in streaks
of green, purple, pinks, pale yellows – the bursting veins
become the sky dancers. The head rolled, weeping.
In the distance the boys watched. When the sky darkened
they ran, bundles bouncing.

aspin tucked us into a buffalo robe,
brushed our cheeks with stained hands. We strained
to see the rib-boned bodies where the heavens explode.
I, *ê-kwêskît*, thought if I ate a passing star
a womb nest of Shakers would love again.

Gone-For-Good's fingers ate spirits and danced.
wâpistikwân built a log-shack of mud and straw.
We lived on rabbit fetuses when *aspin*'s blackness
filled her. White Hair courted snake-hair
truths, they drank from piss-filled bottles. Sold
all our horses, cattle. Lost
our land. Ukrainians hired us to pick sticks
and stones and put up stooks.

Three Person, Mechanic, *ospwâkan*, I, *ê-kwêskît*, *wâpan*,
lost our bundles, wandered the maggot streets,
collected toys from throw away sites. Courted beneath
blankets behind bars.

Three Person made fatherless babies.
They fought for her dangling breasts
and learned to hate men with bad breath.
Mechanic became a stingy recluse,
chopped the tongues off his wives,
his children caged to his pelvis.

ospwâkan hovered at the tree line,
his crooked smile on his sons' lips.
Once in a billion stars we get a glimpse.

I, *ê-kwêskît*, and *wâpan* married white-skinned men,
babies held to our nursing breasts. Rib Woman returned.

Rolling Head gave us her bundles. Slowly
aspin's words unrolled.

wâpan buried Rolling Head and the serpents.
Rosary wrapped around Rib Woman,
she ghost danced, beg danced, guilt danced.
Her strawberry crucified.

Still the story followed.

> kayâs êsa...

And I, *ê-kwêskît*...
At dawn I slipped on thin shoes –
check my rabbit snares,
ask the chickadees, the snow, the sky
if I filled my being with her breath
would I be butchered too? Would I give chase to
what my loins delivered? Would I be spurned?
I kiss the stiff rabbits, throw them over my shoulder.
I peel their fur, wrap them on aspen. My belly full, I
remember the story.

> kayâs êsa ê-kî-mamâhtâwisicik iyiniwak. *Long, long, ago*
> *the people were filled with mystery and magic.*

aspin puffed on her pipe.

> *The head wept. Sang. Rolled. Bumped along*
> *the trodden trails. Their home eaten by fire, flames leaped,*
> *raced toward her. In the distance the boys heard their*
> *mother's terrible cry. They ran. Ran. Ran.*

Hearts raced. Wind burned throats.
Bones bent and stretched. Their mother's breath
at their heels.

I, *ê-kwêskît*, my finger's raced around
the pole, rabbit skin flying.
Eyes dart to fingers, to Gone-For-Good.
Where was I to sleep this night?
aspin's voice was sheets of forest rain,
leaves baking in the ragged wind.

> "âstamik pê-kîwêk. *Come home. Come home.*
> *I love you my babies. My babies. My sons.*"
> *The head begged. Their father's wrath*
> *coiled, held them to their gut. Icy fingers threw*
> *their father's awl. Thorns, rosehips brush,*
> *thistles, brambles, burrs sprung and crowned*
> *the Rolling Head. Hair caught, tangled in these claws.*
> *Rolling Head wept. She struggled, ripped*
> *her face, gouged her eyes. She called. Called.*
> *Still the boys ran, ran, ran.*
> *A fox trotted by, heart filled by the Rolling Head's*
> *wail. He led her through the pass. She rolled. Rolled.*
> *Rolled.* "âstamik nipêpîmak. nikosisak." *Her voice*
> *bee-shit sweet. Still the boys ran.*

aspin took a twig. Relit her pipe.
Saw the story clench my eye,
saw *wâpan*'s inward look.
aspin began....

With severed breath she sang,
"nikosisak, nipêpimak. Come home to your mother's hearth."
The eldest boy threw a flint. Fire sprung behind them.
Rolling Head's face, blistered bacon.
Hair a burnt trail scorched the summer soil.
Her breath a wind of flames at her sons' heels.
Gasping the eldest son turned again. Threw
the rock. Mountains, rocky hills, steep crevices, ravines rose.
She bayed, bayed, bayed.
Rolled back and forth. Back and forth.

I, *ê-kwêskît*, remember how mother, *aspin*, Gone-For-Good,
shot our twenty-two into the sky
whenever she heard a coyote bark, an owl hoot.
Our ears listened for those
creatures of the snowy dark.

aspin slid her hands
down *wâpan's* face,
paused against my cheek.

    Oh the chase, so long, so long.

In teepee, dirt-floor cabin, in the city
the story followed. My memory sniffs
the woven trail.

Gone-For-Good padded the earth,
lifted arms toward the teepee's mouth.
Snowflakes drifted through the parted skin.
She sang for the Rolling Head.

"My babies. My babies. My sons. My little sons.
Come home. Come home. Come home
to your mother's heart."
The boys bled, moccasins eaten by their run.
Bellies empty, eyes swollen, they limped.
Still a beaver's tooth flew, a great river formed.
The boys walked, bellies rolled with water.
They gave themselves to the night.
Across the lake Rolling Head promised
a large water bird marriage if she would spread
its wings. The Swan commanded her to stay still
during the ride or her lonesome bones would
collapse and they would drown.

aspin droned. I, *ê-kwêskît,* my Big Heavens
strained, I straightened my rabbit pole,
laid the fur aside. The skins would be a quilt.

The head clung. Crushed the swan's back. The bird
screeched, flopped and flipped the Rolling Head.
Deep, deep into the black depths, the Rolling Head
became a sturgeon. It flips its tail fin
and devours the river's rotten flesh.

wâpan and I, *ê-kwêskît,* nodded,
sank into the waiting robe.
We did not hear *aspin*'s final words.

In sleep this is where we go.

The embers are starlight
in memory's cave.

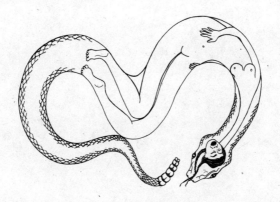

The Promise

When your Big Heavens slumber
the lightning sears
and thunder caresses the prairie
I'll enter your sleep.
Not land, nor water, wind, nor fire,
rock, nor bone, tooth, nor file,
not a fisherman's net, or dream catcher
can impede my good grace.

Some of you will say
But...I never dream.

I will be in your barren walls,
wide-eyed or in your folded sleep
I will be water-borne, the shadow
in your paradise, the fantasy in
your nightmares, the sorcerer
in your illusions, the magician
in your desire.

I will harvest
your bed.

BEHEADING

aspin, mother, nineteen winters
when she married *wâpistikwân*, father.

> *It was* wâpistikwân *who did the marrying.*
> *Not me. Not ever. I had no say.*

In her days parents traded,
bartered, gave away their daughters.

My parents met at boarding school.

> *She wrote love letters,*

my father said.

aspin's mother, *nôhkom*, a French-Cree
large-bosomed woman was *mosom*'s second bride.
Dressed like the French women she studied under.
Ruled the house like the Oblate Sisters.

> *That French Indian attended the reserve's fiddle dances.*
> *Made me wash, starch, iron and stitch ribbons on her Métis*
> *dress. That stingy old bag curled her hair with*
> *aluminum strips. While*
> *I had nothing.*

mosom was a full-blood. A chief
farmer. Taught his daughter
to milk, swirl cream, churn butter,
make cottage cheese, head cheese,
break horses. *aspin*
was her father's son.

> *I was a better horseman than your father. We raced. I won.*

He never forgave me. I wanted to be an army nurse in the
Second World War but that maci-manitow *devil,* kôkom
ruined my life.

My parents loved to square dance, jig.
Three Person, Mechanic, *ospwâkan,*
wâpan and I, *ê-kwêskît,* were born with
their carpet potato knees, suffered
with their limp. Still
we danced.

> *I waited all my life for the love I lost.* pâhpiwiyiniw –
> *Laughing Man from Red Iron. Stingy old bag spooked him*
> *good. I know Onion Man long time. We too had long wait.*
> *And that old bugger, your father, smoke, drank himself – if it*
> *weren't for him these hands would work, feet would still*
> *dance.*

Gone-for-Good watched a spider tumble.
It nestled. Dropped its eggs. Mother incubated them.
All night they hummed:

> *My ring cries, it is said. I wonder if it is true. That is why*
> *I return home.*

aspin's ring finger never ceased throbbing.
After my father left a jeweler cut off the dime store reminder.
Onion Man bought her a copper turtle ring's –

> *If I could breathe I would teach you these –*

short muffled song

> *I never heard it again.*

She told Three Person, *wâpan* and I
she could never see beyond the
crushed chokecherries on granite.

Pounded on a lifeless fridge, a jar
opened her arm. She sucked the juice,
sprinkled sweet sickness, fried the berries
and fed us.

aspin – Gone-For-Good, Little Mother

Knows roots and herbs. Some say
love medicine and bad medicine, too.
I never saw any curses on anyone.
Hers was a bitter-root mouth, though her hands
knew how to help the babies stay.
She used the rosary, met me when I
crawled out of Rib Woman.

> *What you do inside her?*

she'd ask.
She thought living in lairs for days
was suffer she never heard of. She talked like
that. Short, round sentences like her; periods
and commands like the screws and bolts
in her arms. Gone-For-Good, *aspin*,
thinks I look like her. I am taller, plainer.
Mother was once a beauty.

My father, *wâpistikwân*, White Hair, was a looker

> maci-manitow – *the devil lived inside him,*

aspin said. The devil
swished his tail, pounced on her.
We all ran for cover.
Sometimes he was St. Peter, St. Francis Assisi –
squirrels, ducks, rabbit, prairie chicken,
owls ate out of his hand or became pot roast.
Soup mixed with carrots, turnips,
potatoes and cabbage he grew.
I was a puppy,
kneading and sucking White Hair's ear.
Until one day
I, *ê-kwêskît,* was just too old.

Gone-For-Good and White Hair
didn't know I crawled into their skins,
saw all the things they lived and hid.

We'll listen. See through smoke where the dry meat hangs.
nôhkom, Grandmother, built it when *âtayôhkan* thundered.
We'll listen
through this smoke.

THREE PERSON – *nisto-iyiniw*

That was my sister.
She was the first passion before
aspin's ring, built like a mastiff,
her broadside a field of stories.
aspin never forgave her for being born.
aspin's bitter medicine stitched
her mouth. White Hair this.
kôhkom that. Three Person was *aspin*'s
Cinderella, *wâpistikwân*'s dirty poke,
the nuns' pleasure. In marriage a mophead
to *mâtahikan*. She became a pounding board, a cave
where he left his squish.

> *Who got your sewing box? The tread machine?*
> *How much money*
> *did you give to Mechanic? What about* ê-kwêskît?
> *I'm broke.*

aspin retaliated:

> *You're all over the place. You and your thousand*
> *chants and hymns.*
> *Spend uselessly. Trying to be holy in Rib Woman.*
>
> *Her face twisted purple when I give Mechanic*
> *cloth, blueberries*
> *and twenty dollars. She never happy even if she*
> *five hundred winters old.*

The night sun consumed Three Person.
Still, she lifts the blankets,
arranges them on *aspin*,
walks out.

I, *ê-kwêskît*, listened,
watched love wear its boxing gloves.

I, *ê-kwêskît*, THE STORY-SHARER

When I was four-feet tall
my ankle turned against me.
My father told me he'd cut my foot off.
I learned to talk to my feet.

Thick grease flooded the cabin.
I spewed and puked.
My father heaved the frying pan
into the white night.
Father walked. Walked. Walked.
Got a ride to *manawânis*.

nôhkom's skunk lifted its tail
to kill that romantic fever
I suckled from my mother's breast,
my father's enormous ears.

My heart rolled and thrashed,
its finger poked a hole. I still see
through it.

When *mâhtahikan* stood at the door
laughing, my panties at my ankle,
I ran after him
with the slough snakes I captured.

Dark Moon

Rolling Head appeared in the dark moon,
stayed long after Ancient Granny left,
sat on my mother's tailbone,
caused great migraines. With help
from the Old White Man, I, *ê-kwêskît,*
listened. *aspin,* Gone-For-Good's
soul a damp, dark
bundle. She never knew I was there.

> *We gave our children to Indian Affairs.*
> *To the priest. Nuns. The way we were given to god.*
> *A relief to let them go.* wâpistikwân *and I travelled.*
> *Lived and danced in barns, bootlegged their moose milk.*
> *Three Person, the little bastard, became their mother.*
> *We gave Mechanic a twenty-two, tools for his car.*
> ospwâkan *was his father's twin.* ê-kwêskît *calmed my misery.*
> wâpan *came when I was too old to care.*
> *At least I gave them winter stories.*

FROM AFAR I WITNESS

Three Person gave *aspin* a bath last night,
masked *aspin*'s face with Noxema, told her to leave it on.
aspin hard of hearing rasped,

> *Put on my hand-sewn slip so I don't get wet.*

Three Person slipped it over her head,
poked her belly through the torn cloth.
They laughed and laughed as Three Person guided
her into the tub. *aspin* stretched a knee –

> *If it weren't for* wâpistikwân *I'd still be able to...*

she huffed. On haunches she gripped the tub
shifted buttocks, dragged her bent knee.
Three Person shampooed, lifted the basin, rinsed.
Swirled the facecloth on the broad nose. Traced
the tracks on *aspin*'s shoulder.
aspin ached everywhere. English doesn't name
these pains.

> *All the doctors do is give me pills,*
> *and more pills.*

Three Person washes her laundry, makes her bed.
aspin weaves a satin ribbon into her hair
saved from Christmas.

aspin's house was like that.
A packaged valentine chocolate heart hung,
gathered thick dust. Trinkets grandchildren made,
thrown out by parents, decorated shelves.
Faded flowers picked at the graveyard
greet the sun.

Onion Man

I met Onion Man, mother's love,
in a bar while she still wore father's ring.
She hauled me to him
though she doesn't remember.
He was from *wîhcêki-sâkahikan*, Stinking Lake.
A hard-working man whose children
had nothing to do with him.
I thought secrets. Many secrets.
Like us.

Rolling Head lived in the dark moon of *aspin*'s den.
Onion Man snuggled inside. Mute. Waited. Watched.
Years and years.

wâpistikwân bruised her cheeks, dentists replaced
teeth that fell into the toilet, moose milk loosened
her bitter medicine. Doctors plastered her arms,
pinned her legs. She drank Javex. Vomited. Vomited.
Gave herself to the mountains. Threw out my father's
medicine, uncovered her tracks, swept leaves,
pine cones off rotten logs. She bathed in those troughs.
Forty years Onion Man waited.

Beloved and I watched *aspin* barter. A young hunter
selling rabbits a fly couldn't feast on.

> *I'm not paying five dollars for your skeletons,*

she intoned stubbornly.

Onion Man hollered

> *I want the rabbits. It's my business. I'll pay.*

Mother bellowed

> *I want one free, then.*

Young hunter threw the rabbit.

> *Ah, the old people have to see the rabbits first.*
> *Here is a free one.*

aspin hauled it to the sink, hung onto the rabbit's leg.
Sliced the thigh, cracked bone,
peeled the head as if ripping a woman's face.
Cut the ear cartilage, cast the fur. Pried the thighs,
cracked the pelvis, slipped the knife up its rectum,
to the belly, to the nipple of its cage. Pulled the guts.
Trimmed the stomach flaps, removed glands, dug out liver,
the gall bladder. With the rabbit foot she swiped the cavity's
river.

> *I wasn't patient in teaching you the way I taught Three Person.*
> *You were too cranky as a girl. Too impatient.*

I concentrated. Had Mother forgot about the booze?
Fumes that slurred her speech,
her feebleness swiping my uncle off her skirt?
Had she forgotten tiptoeing in the sun-filled shack,
afraid of my father's shadow?
Had she forgotten
how she gave us to bricks and mortar?

Revelations

There is no prayer. Not tonight.
I give in to Rolling Head
though I don't yet know this.
I was in a dream that was all.
Years ago I started this journey –
wandered the woods, talked to trees, the wind,
its creatures. They talked back. I heard a voice
I did not trust, began to see malevolence.
I went to *kêhtê-iyiniw*, the Old Man.
Gave him tobacco. I built Rib Woman.

I saw myself
butchered. Limbs frozen.
Found a finger, a hand, a thigh, a leg.
Searched for my ribs. Lost my heart,
could not see. Lost my head, could not speak.
I did not trust *kêhtê-iyiniw*. So
I went to the dreamer. Rolling Head.
Swam in her skull, gouged and borrowed
her eye, her tongue.
It was the only safe place.

THREE PERSON, *aspin*, *wâpan* AND I

We have walked for centuries.
Mountains, stone hills, pebbles, rocks rolled on top of us.
Squirrels, gophers made cellars, we fell into
their secret meetings. Full bloods making sour milk.
Our ankles cried, complained about their torture. Soles
blistered. Swelled. Marshes hid sands we sunk into,
crawled into all our orifices. We ate rosehips, bramble berries,
raspberries. Strawberries. Vines took root. We came upon a large lake.
Sailors tilted their caps, icebergs gave birth. Still they remained full.

We set our luggage on these islands. Iceberg won't accept our fare.
Breaks its head. *aspin* and I jump, land on her heart. Three Person
is cautious. Terrified. *wâpan* falls. We drag her up. Iceberg bobs,
threatens to crack. Three Person jumps, frozen fingers grab her dress.
aspin snips her free. We leave our luggage, enter the lodge of a crude
village
where our relatives smoke meat. Village dancers in garbage bags.
A woman wants to jingle dance, her spirit won't lift a foot.
I roll her in a blanket. *Breathe,* I command.
The voice answers, *I want to hatch.*
I recognize him though it doesn't register. Not right away.
I lay my dark body, fire-lighting his hypothermic heart.
He's mercurial. I've learned to read creatures and he is clear to me.

> *I like you. I like you very much. I like everything*
> *About you. It's nothing to put up with you,*

he confessed. Still he was abrasive, buried his face in
the *Globe and Mail.*
I give him the finger.

He was startled by the snake that jumped on his lap.
Emerald, frisky snake. Provocative, though he doesn't see anything.
Strawberry vines bind us. He tells me,

> *I feel we've met before. A former life, perhaps.*
> *But yes, how foolish of me. I should know your face anywhere.*

I knew this since the heavens opened.
The sky flew, became a placenta eater,
swam into the future, straight to the womb.
I pushed sage behind my ear,
shoved it into my eyeballs.
Placed several sticks in his pocket.

> *One day you will sing,*

I tell him. He sings like an oriole.
Mellow longing. Lips mussels
on the ocean's belly. He is mute,
scared of his own song.

I never tire of his talks.
And my sister and mother,
they had their haunts.

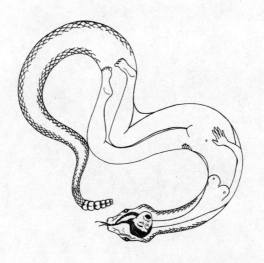

Many Loves Have I – *ê-kwêskît*

My Beloved is a Scotsman.
A hillside stone covered in lichen,
a prairie bench to rest on. His Big Heavens
are the flash of a hummingbird, penetrating.
Once his jaws clamp,
he cannot be moved. His baseball-gloved
hands held our babies
as if he was banding fledgings.
Fifty years his universe anchored
in my lair.

Yet. Magpie stole my heart.
I saw his tracks. Stalked him.
And when I turned he was beside me.
This one, Rolling Head said,

> *Pick your lover out of your skin.*

His medicine wedged,
attached to my head, wormed into my sleep,
swam in my womb.
I burned and burned. He was like that.
Big Heavens swallowed my lips, my landscape.
How my belly shook.
I had nowhere else to put him.

My Beloved and my Obsession
hunger for my skin, papers,
books, earth, music, song. Although
none of us fit anywhere,
we were everywhere.

Snakes scare *aspin*,
Three Person's milk flowed in the fields.

She ran, found a snake slithering
toward her child. Chopped its head.

wâpan goes to confession, like Mary,
snakes at her feet.
Mechanic is a snake.
And I, *ê-kwêskît*?
We are *nôhkom*'s necklace.

DAMN HIM. DAMN HIM.

I've known Magpie many years.
Appearing when I was the least interested,
when I thought
I had worked him out of my life,
he'd arrive. Watch behind this tree and that,
tempt me with his slender illustrious tail –
cocking, fluttering it, he mocked
with his devious eyes.
Oh, for so long,
the cavern he pecked from my strawberry
remained raw and wounded.
Oh, how I wanted him then.

WHITE ISLAND

Rolling Head took me for a stroll.
My boots and pants soaked
from last night's rain, slipped
on lichen, my foot wedged.
Rolling Head guided me to
a coyote's den, this
became my lair.

There,

she said,

you will pick your lover out of your skin.

For years I dug through that coyote's tunnel.
The water ship of childhood dreams
emerged as I struggled to surface.
When my head peered through
mother's hole,
a heat of bullets,
the rolling thunder of wheels
seared over me.
I slipped back into that muddy place.

I had not yet heard
about the battles my ancestors fought.
Yet
through my youth
I followed my Beloved's green eyes.
He carried my grandfather's stature,
leaned into the land
his ancestors bought for ten dollars in
1912.

But
Rolling Head swallowed my lover and me.
In her cavity
we made love,
sweating to tear our skins apart.

I have a white island
on my left hip
I share with my Beloved,
foreigner on my brown nakedness.
Though I've made love with my lover
I've never touched
his flesh.

In the Place of Wisdom

Beloved and I share a pine branch.
We fill a jar with sweet needles. Later
it will be smudge. A prayer like
his mouth against mine. Some time ago,
skiing, my boots bit into my bone,
left dollar size bruises. He wrapped
a tea towel. He would not leave without me.
Over rapids he coached every stroke. We dipped,
flew through the woods. Trees waved. An eagle
supervised. We pitched our tent where a boulder
lifted its thick moss head, craned to look at us,
and said,

> *"Oh, it's you."*

I sprinkled tobacco
in the water, laid it under its back.

Magpie he is the other. I won't share his name.
nika-kiyâskin. I'd lie if I did. Never mind.
His bird-like claws
held the cappucino. One whisky-jack heaven
enters mine. The other shifty eye deep, already lost.
In flames he sings,

> *"What's love got to do with it?"*

I dig out the "The Art of War."
The table lifts, dangles its feet, thumps,
rattling saucers, coffee cups. The bench quivers.
Magpie says,

> ê-kwêskît, *your calmness is everybody's excitement.*
> *Wherever you go, everybody loves you.*
> *The Old Man told you*

you'd meet like minds and like hearts.
Beloved and I must not hold you.
Go. That is your journey.

A speech so long,
he never gave it again.

A TREK

Through the coat of winter,
backpacks heavy,
we watched the flare,
our mitten thumbs
clenched.

 I've sat in my grandfather's sled going to midnight mass,
 in hay and layers of blanket. Stars laughed as the horses plowed,
 bells shattered the snow.

The reserve and Alberta borders
were all I knew. Wrapped in
wool and down,
Beloved and I were going East.

 In the mountains we were otters sliding
 on one another in the Whiterabbit River's April thaw.
 His skin bone-snow. Mine mud-river.

After I'd warmed from miles
of exhausting cold, a night's sleep
on boughs, my Beloved wiped my frozen face,
murmured soon
we'd be through Toronto. I faced
the traffic West,
determined to return to Rib Woman.

 In a tarp-covered kitchen
 wâpistikwân explained in Cree
 the give-away of his youngest
 to this green-eyed stranger.
 I, his translator.

I waited in a café

of my Beloved's home town.
He'd be back to pick me up, he said,
if all went well. I am the give-away,
a daughter of the country
in a mountain marriage.

Voices wailed inside.
Love no matter how deep
has its penalties.

A woman ran up the stairs
singing muffled songs of her wayward son.
The song clung to each step
as if a church
organ broke from strain.

We loaded the stoneboat with my meager belongings.
Hiked *aspin's* crutches and lifted her brokenness. She saw
beyond trees, over mountains. The woods witnessed this
wedded walk.

The table is set with finery. I've seen
this in the rectory of nuns and priest.
My Beloved's jaw is clenched.
I am the only one who sees. The man
leans and asks,

"What does your father do?"

I watched my father White Hair's lovely burnt muscle
lift the sugar beet hoe as he laboured in the excited sun.
For a penny or two he skinned,
stretched beaver. Walked in thundering cold
to find a ride to the sick building.
I lay soaked in whooping cough.

My English is not good enough.
I answer,

> *"My father*
> *is a common labourer*
> *and lives on skid row."*

nôhkomak's voices keep interrupting, eager
to have their say. I see them, give-away brides
starry-eyed as I, as they trudged behind
their fur-trader husbands.

My Beloved lies beneath my neck.
He breathes slowly, gently.
Flesh between my legs shifts.
I gather him, blend his body
back into mine.

> *"Indian girls. Indian girls. Oh how I love those Indian girls."*

nôhkom wore beads, gems, silk, an Englishman's bride.
Poured tea from pewter. Served the governor duck she
caught while bathing. In Indian summer she donned her
bustles, stripped off her gloves, conjured the nightly spirits,
fed the dead. Called all her relatives to feast.

In the eastern swelter my belly grew.
Our newborn blessed by water.
I went home for a burial. I wasn't gone
a day when a blonde sweetheart called
my Beloved. I remember the country marriages.
Governor Simpson disposed of his Indian bride.

Oh yes, *nôhkom* carried her newborn, horseback riding
through the mountains with her factor. Her people
supplied his men with ponies, winter kill, dried buffalo,
pemmican, and berry-wraps. Through the storms the gentle
Cree thawed the foreign tribes. In the sun-skinned night the
traveller mapped the rivers, lakes, mountain pass.

The sun twisted, exploded,
butchered my womb.
Our second newborn received a welfare burial
the day Beloved started school.

One Fabien sent his half-breed son to the seminary.
He travelled Europe dressed like an English lord, he spoke
his tribal *nêhiyawêwin*, English and French. Came home and
died a Cree.

pimîhkân arrived in the mail.
The sickness of the lost tongue
stole my sleep. I hung a swing
outside a tree, watched
our first born grow. "Cowboys
and Indians" round and round,
a pistol in his chubby hands.
Heard my *kôkom* whisper

"I'd give my spirit to be back among my people."

Another middleman married the half-breed daughter
of a dark-skinned mother, raised on a trapline, cultured
in fine manners, many languages too. Became a lady of
the fort, a baroness in the frontier.

Did you see the rainbow fall?
Another child was born with a musical smile
and pony legs. Two babies straddle
the rainbow. Two faces moved
toward the fallen sun. A tailwind
spun our hearts. A man, a woman,
watched our lights disappear.

I hear my grandmother,

"Oh, my daughter I see you go. Your father walked many
miles behind the whipping storm while I pushed to give
you sun. I placed you against my breast. Know my child,
the mountains make your dreams. Keep decent and proper.
Serve your guest tea, scones. Never forget you're Cree."

A story awoke. Onion berry-smoked voices
spoke. Bones, pottery and polished silver fought.
Hockey, theatre, ballet strutted while Rib Woman
waited. The symphony bowed to beaded dresses,
still my drum called. The bible praised. An airplane
flew east. *aspin* in her reserve home waited.
Beloved and I fed our babies stone-ground bread,
bannock and lard.

There are only shadows. *nôhkom* never had her
say. Ear on tree I listen to the sap. It burns my
veins, wakes the very wild. I lift *nôhkom*'s dark
face. Her voice whistles winter winds, awakens the
sleeping day, painted thunder in the summer sun. I
suckle the still water of an offered breast.

Beloved and I have arrived.
One child lives his namesake,
Birds that Fly Between Heavens.
The other dips,
steams the rocks, follows the Rainbow.
A grandson plays the violin,
the other has a piano in his heart.
My Beloved has become my flesh.

> "My daughter, whom I love tenderly, see that you
> live in the world of peace, tranquility, and
>
> contentment, all the days you shall live...See that
> you honour me and your father, reflect glory on us
> by your good life."[2]

There is no stillness in the autumn rain.
nôhkom carried her smoke in her apron,
peppermint on the breath of the lunar moon.
mosom traces syllabics, through my fingers.
And my Beloved?
We are his earth.

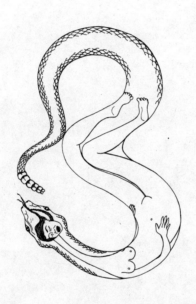

mâmaskâc – AMAZING!

Big Heavens concentrate.
The road opens,
eats our car.
Mother, *aspin,*
with unreserved passion, wove this...
My ears pencilled
and I record.

> *"I was scrubbing clothes at the trough, dress tied to my waist.
> Sweating when Onion Man arrived. I had not seen him since
> boarding school. Since I married. My heart ran. I'd been changing
> sheets, scrubbing toilets at a resort. We waited so long."*

> *"When wâpistikwân, that bastard
> broke the mirror, sliced my arm. I left."*

We travelled.
Rolling Head wove *aspin's* dream.

She worked her jeans over scarred legs. Shoved her bunion-
twisted foot into her cowboy boots. Beneath her bed, she
retrieved her moccasins, remembered the mingy tenderness of
wâpistikwân, my father, and laughed. Lifted the tarp to her
makeshift kitchen, slipped quietly out. *aspin* stood by the
sîpiy. *"Where are you going?"* it asked. She loosened the Irish
twist, sprinkled it into the yawn. *Swallow these, rip them
against jagged rocks, make them nameless, they are sickness.* The
moccasins sobbed as they flew into the thundering arms.

aspin raced toward the stone hills, jumped across a fat stream,
placed her foot in the lips of the cliff, its eye, its ear. Boots
wounding. She climbed. Sucked in frigid breath. An
old woman handed her a kerchief, she hauled herself up.
They never said a word. My mother knew where she must go.

aspin smeared charcoal on her bottom lids – *like a football player*, she laughed. The mountain would recognize her. Ambushed bones lay beneath, they will not disturb her. She picks a pimpled severed doll's head. An eye turns inward, the other stares.

The head rolled
in our jalopy. I have found one
like it. We know
Rolling Head's touched us,
though I haven't figured out how.

That summer Mother, Three Person, *wâpan* and I
attend a Parch Dance. *wâpan* dances. Starves. Bleeds
for us. Now and then *aspin*'s knees flutter.
The dreamers drag skulls, fall under the blistered sun.
Flesh pierced, some hang beneath the ribbon tree.
We trilled when a dream is freed.
Exorcism, lost loves, life, left at the bleeding tree.

I watched *aspin* wander. Wanted smoked meat. That
day she was a cougar, youthful for a short time. Too long
caught in steel, neck severed, belly sliced. A lonely
confusion of hide, rags, prison cloth, large beads.
She hid shattered desire. Mouth parched, squealing in mid
death, her Rib Woman left with one wet drop.
In wee hours she clung to the down mattress as if he, Onion
Man, lay there.

nêhiyânâhk

Car hoods, tires, bicycle wheels, glass, leaning shacks.
Sweat lodge ribs, fragrant trees still wrapped
from last year's offerings.
Wild dogs, laughing, singing brown faces.
Moose nose, duck soup, berries, coke, pizza.
Sweet grass blessed all.
Three Person and I slip on warty masks, broken spectacles,
scarves, shawl hunch our backs, build massive buttocks.
Flower skirts cover pot-bellies, socks layer our stockings.
We enter *tawinikêwin* in lopped off rubbers and canes.
Drummer sings. We sway, bounce the hips of young bucks,
goose those in the way. Soon we will all be bone-lean,
wide-eyed, filled with Rolling Head.
But
none of us know this.

wîhtikow sâkahikan – nêhiyânâhk

Beloved and I drive in silence to *nêhiyânâhk,*
pass hills, clustered aspen, slow to watch a nursing deer.
I etch my Beloved's face, slide down his arm.
He lifts my hands to his lips, on my thigh.
We often touch. In snores between dreams,
buttocks, thighs, legs entwined.
He avoids a bloated porcupine. I inhale the air.
Skunk medicine awakens the romantic fever. I
don't share this.
Sometimes I am Beloved's Big Heavens,
turn the steering wheel
off an oncoming ditch. His fingers drum,
punch the air. I don't hear,
don't ask.

Ceremony. It has begun. I offer tobacco
to the Standing People. I address the directions.
wâpanohk, âpihtâ-kîsikânohk. pahkisimotâhk. kîwêtinotâhk.
My axe severs the willows. I am scratched,
burdocks cling everywhere.
All the dreamers choose bush sites. Bend, bend –
willows shoved into the earth.

At the homesite. I made a fire in our tent.
When I returned
The plastic frames were bent. *kêhtê-aya*
laughed. Laughed.

> *"He ate a moose from its nose to its arse for her.
> And she bragged about how smart this green-eyed
> man is."*

He never forgot that.

At dusk the dreamers sat in the large
roundness of Rib Woman. A bird choir,
bees, frogs sang. After bannock,
stew, berries, water, the choir
followed the going-away.

In the Darkness of the Rolling Head

In the curved breast of the hills
Three Person and I, and the rest of the dreamers,
wide-eyed share a story or two.
We leave spaces. Infinite spaces.

The succession works.

Three Person pulled the tarp,
tied herself into the buffalo robe and slept.
Before the first bird sang someone
grabbed her ankles.
She clawed the bodiless fingers. Broke free.
Clutched her chest, contorted, she grabbed a fist.
Sobs heaved. Mucus ran. In lucid moments,
she noticed teeny spiders skate on the globs.
Bunched grass. Rolling Head is mounds of earth,
standing wood, a cricket. Three Person
was with *pâhkahkos*, on the road to deliver
poultice to the sufferers. *pâhkahkos* jeered in her ear.
Problems were medicine.
When she got a flat tire. It was medicine.
When she didn't get a job. It was medicine.
When she got sunstroke. Medicine.
When the bingo passed her. Medicine.
Drank Buckley's. Polysporin wormed her cuts.
Antibiotics gave her trots. White man's medicine.

Maybe it was Onion Man, *aspin*,
mâtahikan, perhaps her old lover Delicious
Fork. Maybe her heart-eating children. So
many curses. Over and over Rib Woman
played back her projector.

I, *ê-kwêskît*, don't know if Three Person
walked through the dark.

FOLDED IN RIB WOMAN

I, *ê-kwêskît,* am folded in Rib Woman.
The ground digs.
Thin blanket flattened. Hips bruised.
Muscles will not unfold.
I kneel, lower my head, attempt to sleep.
I scratch dirt, grovel, inhale
her sweet moistness. The moon's thick
face peers in. Heat between my thighs.
So hot. I do not burn. So hot.
No blood. No. Taste my fingers.
Nectar dry. I have been dead so many years.

EXCAVATING

I, *ê-kwêskît,* share this story,
though a small pain only.

Shadow dancers arrived, ran on Rib Woman's
roundness. Twigs fall. Thunder rolls. A
dead tree slaps Rib Woman. She
heaves through the night. Breathes, breathes.
Hours. Hours. Many, many nights.
Years. Years. Time and time again.
Rolling Head dreams. Mouth parched.
Tongue thick.

Obsession. Obsession. Obsession.
Over and over I leave him here.
Friends, that is all.
My rock has four heads
I found at Holy Lake. I smudge, cradle,
and sleep with it. This is my Beloved,
our children. I show my want.
A treaty. Yes, a treaty.
Still
hungry heavens bend, breathe me.
Knees stagger from this whorish inflammation.
He walked away from another. He doesn't
reveal names. I know, say her name.
A storm, red, black flushed. I've gone too deep.
Inheritance at work.
Swallow this bitter root.

THOU SHALL NOT COVET

I won't do this any more –
pretend I can pluck stars
from the eagle's eye.
I won't sit on branches
croaking, preening my body.
I won't lick my lips
as if I am a woman rutting.
I won't lie,
not any more.

I can tell you this –
I'll blow chains into your mouth,
loop them over your ear,
string them to your nipple.
When I pull
you'll never run again.

You won't shame me
with your lustful tongue.
I'm the mouth that holds
your honey,
day after day at your desk,
in your dream before sleep
beside your woman's body.

I'm not pretending
I don't know the way your jeans
hug your forward movement.
The way you drag your feet.
The way you erase your heat.
I'm not in a pigeon dance,
waiting for
the prairie cock's blind thumping.

I won't be coy
as I blow the woman's wind,
scatter your seed into my night,
bring them to my finger, mouth,
while you torch your woman.
I in my cotton night.

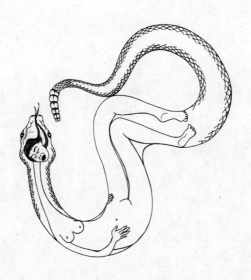

ê-kwêskît 'awâsis êkwa nôtokwêsiw'

I am old. Old.
I've devoured my eggs
every mating moon. Lost my memory,
nôhkom drove me crazy. Sleepless nights,
she becomes Tammy Wynette, sings

> *"You're the reason I don't sleep at night,"*

leaves me with belly aching laughter.
I want to tell Obsession this.

I never said I was sane.
I share this story as I witnessed it.
Listen for Chrissake –

nôhkom rose high, filled the forest lodge.
Showed many pages of her face:
awâsis êkwa nôtokwêsiw.
She arrives nightly, this bleeding sun
feather-mists over my breast,
scarred belly and seared thighs.
Stretches at dawn, shifts her wrinkles
to close one sun
(the other a wide-eyed heaven).
My *nôhkomis.*

wâpan – DAWN

Crazy cradles me, *ê-kwêskît.*
Maybe you've figured it out.
Cradles *aspin*, Three Person,
Mechanic, *wâpan.*
I love Crazy's
insane laugh. She doesn't
believe a word I've written.

wâpan, a child of a hundred fathers.
That is our secret. *aspin*, mother,
doesn't know we've figured it out,
but it doesn't matter.
wîhtikow sâkahikan is filled
with children like her, though
she's no longer a child.
Poor *wâpan*. I loves her silly.

aspin calls Three Person's children

> *Loose shoe, one shoe, five shoe*

as if Gone-For-Good, *aspin*'s never been a loose woman.
Her bitter root spews,

> *Sperm donors, that's all she collects.*

In Rib Woman, *wâpan* lies naked.
Sun-baked, prune-like, she feels
a presence. A faceless Old One.
He cuts little xs diagonally at her feet,
criss-crossing her belly, breast, arms.
No pain. No bleed. She remembers *aspin*'s
buffalo horn sucking. The flint
under the Sun Dance Tree. Old One

is without a knife, a razor, or flint.
The cuts pucker, full mouths blowing kisses.

Arms on her midriff she rises. Sings. Bursts
into laughter. Old One comes behind,
pushes her forward. She knows she can
stop the fall, chooses not to. Falls,
still laughing. Other dreamers sliced
the same way. She recognizes a dreamer
playing with blocks. Kneels. Joins him.

I, ê-kwêskît, don't tell her what
her thought doesn't see. It is not my place.

THE VISIT

His laughter is winter gravel,
sprays all within reach.

I am used to a ball cap,
stained jeans, earth-filled nails.

He crawls culverts, swims rivers,
drags out the bloated. Thaws
the stiffs. Kneels in
charcoal with a dinner fork,
lifts flesh, blistered skin. Under
a lamp he lays fragments.
Stitches later, his smudge-stained
pages rise to their feet. He feels their stare,
hears their talk, their fingers at his spine.
He snaps to their command.

We feasted, he and I.
Carrion left us no choice.
We were told
there aren't enough of us anymore
to make the dead cry.

The White Goddess

I suppose you think it weird
that I'd give my sister Three Person
this name. We are like that on the rez.
Like me, *ê-kwêskît*, my real name is
Chatterbox. Rubber Mouth. It might as well
Be Diarrhea. But really...
I am Bernadette. Christianized. Colonized.
Confirmed. Bernadette. Don't tell
anybody. I like *ê-kwêskît* better.

My ears hear crazy things. But
I am crazy (they tell me) so
what does it matter whether
you believe me or not. It's not important.
Enjoy your coffee. Don't put too much
sugar. Listen.

White Goddess, Three Person,
was the Hunchback of Notre Dame.
Her body crowded her, just like the ten thousand
chants and hymns she gave birth to.
I am seventy. Yes. Let's see, she'd be
eighty-five if she was still standing.

When she met our cousin's
white husband, a good Christian,
the first time, he wiped his nose.
Remember? He did that to me too.
Poor Three Person.

No one knows *wâpistikwân* dug
into her diapers. How he goaded her
as if she was a donkey. In wood chopping.
Hauling water. Washing floors. Dishes.
He never left their side: *aspin*,
Three Person, and Mechanic.

When *wâpistikwân* went to the farms
life was still. Until drunk with panty remover,
the welfare cheque gone,
darkness came down.

One day Three Person told *aspin*
her sin. *aspin* screeched. Told her not to lie.
Struck her with a cast iron frying pan.
Left a bald spot.

Three Person showed me her ring

> *"I married Christ in boarding school,*
> *filled with the heart of Mary. He left me too.*
> *When I was married off to* mâtahikan,
> *I was happy to leave.* mâtahikan *climbs on me every*
> *night. Too many bastards, aspin said."*

THE HOUSE OF BITTER ROOT – *wîhkês*

Buckley's stops the cough,
wîhkês cures it.
The old people encouraged me, *ê-kwêskît,*
to take both.

Romantic fever grabbed clumps of hair,
stuck a needle in Three Person's head.
The White Goddess could not sleep,
dug a worm from her heart.
Still the heart walked. Walked.
Snake blinked its sweet tongue.

A child's ear leaked.
Another was strangled by invisible hands.
A son robbed a daughter's night.
White Goddess did not see,
so twisted in the sweet tongue.

> *"At* mâtahikan*'s deathbed scrawny hands gripped me. I
> beat him when he was done. Forgive me. I wanted to make
> sure his hands would never reach beyond the grave. I shall
> never sleep. Never sleep."*

Horse Liniment and The Boys

The old people wear that smell.
I think to kill Father-What-A-Waste.

I've gathered this from Mechanic,
this before *ospwâkan* left,
this before *wâpistikwân*, my father, lived.
Make of it what you will,
this story.

> *I am called* wiyipiyiniw, *filthy man, a bastard.*
> *Because of me mother will stay in hell. To all*
> *of you bunch of bitches* – pisikwâtisak, *mens*
> *are bastards.*

> *I was shipped to St. Judas. Spoke little English,*
> *hid my Cree. Cut my braids. I thought someone died.*
> *I wanted charcoal to paint my cheeks. Father-What-A-Waste*
> *became a hornet, unbuckled his belt. My breath ran those*
> *hallways. I fought. His neck was a cobra. Sister threw ice water, a*
> *scrub brush, lye soap. I burned. Forced cod-liver oil.*
> *I vomited and vomited. Licked the floor.*
> *Sacred old man buggered me. Bastards. How can I share this?*

wâpistikwân, my father, Mechanic,
they were never sorry.
ospwâkan on his knees
by the toilet.

A Sane Leaving

Sometimes I entered their hearts,
blew the family embers.
The flame consumes us all.
Threw water.
It dragged us under. Created dreams.
The wind was forgotten.
I just wanted my last breath.
Still the story, always the story...

aspin makes her marks on walls. Greets all her decorations
as if they were live companions.

A cracked moon greeted all her guests. Bone-shell earring swayed
as she looked over. When she approves, her sour face invites you in.
Today Mother wore a white tam, plaid sweater, blue blouse,
polka dot brown flowered dress. Green leggings, lime socks
and hush puppies. She clung to a black purse, her cane, a bottle of pills.

Acorn man hovered over brewed thick tea.
A bald British man's smoke-stained beard
touched the floor. He followed the burnt smell of raisin rice.
aspin changed his cranberry, fir boughs,
according to the seasons.

A knotted wrinkled woman peers from deep cheekbones.
Nose bends west. Jaw half-eaten, ready to laugh,
she clutched a fleshing tool and scraper.
A fly lifted its greasy feet on her spotty horse-hair head.

In the bedroom walnut man smirked, listened to a "difficult time"
as people smudged over him.

Saucers of pebbles, mismatched earrings, batteries, snakeskin,
dried lizards, frogs, sit on her dresser. She's draped a satin shawl
across the skunk pelt. Northern lights dance across the fabric.

aspin observed all this. Hollowness embraced her.
She purled and dropped. Onion Man arrived, stepped
on the forest shavings. *aspin* dropped her knitting,
tended the woodstove, poked the jelly roll.
She remembered the second-hand veil, photographed
wedding. Her want at the river's edge. His scent lingered.
wâpistikwân had noticed their smiles, sideward glances.

Yet, *wâpistikwân* was handsome, large mouth delicious, stories
stretched his secret voice.
She blamed his mother for her prison.
When they were married, she guarded her thoughts,
covered her blotched face with creams. Hands grew inward.
She averted her eyes for fear they'd run.
Her hip threw her walk. Three Person thought *aspin*
spent too much time at the bedbug mansion wearing
rejected skins, though *aspin* poured lye, sure she thought
she'd killed the spirits.
Still *aspin* became someone we didn't know.
She'd gyrate, ridicule others,

> *I wonder if* kiskânak *is still alive. She was crazy.*

Mother would stand with hands on hips,
watch us drive away. A woodpecker
at her head.

> *It was a wonder that my thinking doesn't leak.*

Outside a battered tea kettle hangs on a poplar elbow.
A charcoal frying pan leans into the ashes.

Trees stand alert.
Just her, this endless hollowness.

UNDERCURRENTS

nôhkomak met me at the rapids.

Dive deep and gather,

they said.
From the darkness water people emerged.
Stories they gave
I could not read. I could not hear.

We launched our canoe,
followed the arrow
through the rapids.
No time to be afraid: arms out, drawing.
Reaching.

The water against our shell
lifts us onto her rolls and throbs.
Our paddles stick against her embrace.

I am filled,
to be swallowed by water, wide awake,
breathing her.

Dive deep and gather,

they insisted.

Dance this new language.

TEEPEE LINING

Endometriosis hounded me all my life.
A ball of snakes came alive
every moon
when my love drummed
the log.
They left when Age arrived.

I coughed: a ball of blond, auburn, red, black,
brown and grey tumbled out. Strand after strand.
The color of my hair changed with each worried breath:

> *I am a worrier. You devoured me as if I was a tart*
> *raspberry. Worried about how you'd pay your Visa,*
> *buy books, birdfeed, dog food, gas.*

One said,

> *I'm the blond, your part-time skunk. Your buddy, you*
> *wondered if you'd ever see that cross-eyed boy who kept*
> *you awake.*

Black hair claimed me for its sight. This I tore out
when my babies consumed spirits,
emptied their bellies at our door.
Another said,

> *Red, here, crashed your car when Beloved offered fawn-*
> *eyed woman a lift without you.*

Autumn strand arrived after my stillborn.
Whitie fell out when I saw my father *wâpistikwân's*
birthday weep.

My hair is wild,
is in my face, each strand
demands I listen:

> *Burn us when the moon fills your belly. Braid us for*
> *your lodge. Sing.*

A bear staggered, snorting hard
up the hill. Head lolling. I listened.
Goose bump jumped. Bear stopped.
I cradled her skull, a plate everyone eats from –
filled her crevices with sage and sweet grass.
She arrived from the North, sat at the mouth
of Rib Woman. Her cubs came in,
nuzzled me in my sleep.

What are these?
Snakes, birds, wings, skulls,
bear, deer, stones that live inside me?
What use are they
that make the dead laugh, the living cry?

SCARECROW

On a washboard highway
I saw a hide hitchhiking. I made a wild u-turn,
pulled alongside. Traffic picked up.
I pulled out a map, listened to my ear,
as mother said about the cellphone.
I grabbed hide's arms, legs, flung
her into my pickup. I shoved
the ill-bathed hitchhiker into a bag.
I'll make a purse, a doll, a needle case.
Baskets.

I sit on the ground, slice the arching belly,
of the moose's leg, give her a C-section.
The leg chatters

> *The butcher discarded me as if I've never served*
> *a purpose. As if I've lost all life.*

The moose hide slides down,
smiles

> *I want colorful, shiny beads. Up and down my torso.*

Curls around my feet.

Knees bent and spread, a pole
hugs my thighs. I stretch, scrape
the skin on metal. Hide squeals.
Groans.
A cross-eyed, plastered waxwing
drunk on mountain ash,
watches. Slurs to its relatives
about the butchering. They decide
to shit on my glasses next time I
walk beneath them.

SWEET SICKNESS

Three Person followed Sweet Tongue.
He moved inside her bowels.
When he spoke, spittle flew.
Mesmerized, wet lips lay deep
in other sweet-eyed bitches. Home a day or two,
he filled her hunger. Her strawberry blossomed.

Cigarettes burned her arms, she clawed
her head. Porcupine quills, raspy tongue
scraped her insides. No comfort with salves.
She made offerings, ribbons, she begged
the therapist to suck her temples.
Sweet love drove her mad.

> *Sweet love took seed*
> *to hell where I rot,*

she said.

POSSESSED

aspin, our mother, doesn't know
we followed her footsteps.
One day she told me
she heard I broke a marriage.

I had told him this –

> *You've done this to me.*
> *Dressed me like a dragonfly,*
> *fed me fat mosquitos,*
> *held a lady mantis, silky tongue,*
> *licked my swollen wings.*
> > *Fly*
> *you told me, as if she-wolves have wings.*
> *I hang from the thistle*
> *of your bone. Prayed*
> *I would not be crushed by the passerby.*
>
> *I've set my feet*
> *on tracks I thought were yours.*
> *Chanting* nôhkom*'s song,*
> *I followed you.*
> *The same hunt as my father's shadow,*
> *Mother's splintered bones.*
> *Your glacial heat burns*
> *these sin-filled needs*
> *as I search for your spirit wings.*
>
> *I've purged this last day,*
> *tongue on the kettle of the winter sun.*
> *I'll make love in the belly*
> *of* wîhtikow*'s winter lair.*
>
> *You've done this to me.*

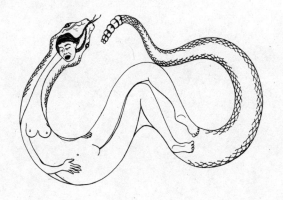

The Tracker

A guitar strums,
fingers caress the chords.
Ears listen. The musician walks the alley.
I met him. I was bending into the wind.
Ice glares. He hears my sobs.
Lifts my hood, kisses my cheek.
The twang shatters the window,
frost spreads like fire rolling in snow.
The music is rhythmical. Hair falls on
his forehead...

> *I am sad for all that has happened. This fire*
> *leaves a crater too deep to fill. Tell me what to do,*
> *ê-kwêskît, tell me what to do. You've torn my skin.*
> *I am a narrow miss in the traffic, still trembling.*
> *I am a slow learning as I go.*

My room is filled with unruly books.
I watch him watching me as I drop my clothes.
Scars on my belly. Waist wattled,
swaddled, spills. I don't hide anything.

His murderous want to possess me.
He deposits my decapitated head in plastic,
wraps my limbs in a brown bag.
Brings me to a barn, lays me in a freezer.
Marked as hamburger.

I memorize his moves. Know his mouth.
His thoughts. His feelings. His doings.

I suffer Beloved too.
He moves next to me, snores in my ear.
I clasp his bum.

Romantic fever runs in my family.
Men's. Women's.
A catching disease.
Too many years of grieving
in Rib Woman, Rolling Head laughing.
I am surrounded by shakers in
this mud-water.

Rolling Head is hookworm.
I regurgitated her when I was snowshoeing.
Snow woman shifted between skins.
Her face ghostlike, nun cropped hair,
hips gyrating, she thrust her mound.
I dipped my finger.

HER MANY FACES

The watcher travels the cold path.
I am a fool climbing these endless stairs.
Rolling Head coaches from a branch –
a breast on bark suckles,
her face sleeps beneath a luscious trunk.
Willow pregnant, she cradles her child.
That is all. That is all.
Who am I to speak for her?

Still
the watcher yearns to give form,
a waiting bush trail worn out by
boots that crush her lungs. Stud-metals bite,
sandals chafe her skin,
sneakers spring her awake, her breasts' sour
thickness runs. She lies, as the mindless walk.

She brushes against the pretty girl, clings
to her sweater. The girl looks, doesn't see.
She slaps the broad hunched man, stings his startled
face. Giggles. At times outstretched hands cradle
squirrels, offer them to a camera,
brags a singsong,

"See."

She peers from a basket, a sly eye.
The watcher watches the watched.
Ecstasy arches behind doors. Computers
listen, crawl long lines, wait for the sorrow.
Walls, floorboards stand guard, record
their daily pace. The watcher stretches,
sore and swollen.

MY TEACHERS

The Old Man would say,

> *I was dinking in my head.*

Hand pointed to Rib Woman,

> *This is our psychology.*
> *All the answers are inside you,*
> *everything you need. Dink for yourself.*

When I, *ê-kwêskît*, still wanted clarity,
the Old Man
would open his palms,

> *Let's check out the policy.*

Still I wanted to know.

The Old White Teacher
often asked,

> *What do you think?*

I wanted to hit him.

The Old Indian Woman
advised

> *Part your Big Heavens:*
> *all is there.*

The Old White Woman
wanted to know,

What are you feeling?

Then him. Obsession.
Pulling my entrails and scabby tripe,
halitosis burning my face.
He would plead,

> *Be gentle with me. Be gentle with me. I am fragile.*

wîhtikow hibernates.

The Old Man told me,

> *Your Beloved loves you more than life.*

I'd wash Beloved's feet,
manicure all his nails.
Massage his body.
Leave him in a spasm of rest.

ê-kwêskît PANDORA

Today I opened a box.
I wanted to know what I'm made of.

Stones. Feathers. Bones. Skins.
I don't understand this.
I greet each one as they caress
my face, my fingers, my eyes –
lay them tenderly in order, size, family.

Coyote, bear, deer, fox,
mallard, raven, owl, chickadee,
weasel, mouse, rabbit, squirrel.
Bones. Jaws. Vertebrae. Ribs.
Wings. Tails. Claws. Teeth.
Bats, frogs, newts, butterflies.
Dried spiders.
Walrus stone. *mitêwiwin* pebbles.
Stones with eyes. Jagged crystals.
Fur. Snakeskins.

nôhkom's grinding. Powder floating.
Sweet root standing, sweet root hanging.
The bear that lives in me.

These intricate dead – Memento Mori.
The priest said,

> *I've made my peace,*

as he lifted a fork of charcoal bodies,
my ancestors' bundles, sacred pipes,
braided hair and pelts.

The intricate dead,
my love.

A turtle's heart
beating hours and hours
after she is dead.

SNOW SNAKE AND WINGS

I watched Snow Snake
stand on a platform of feeding flames.
She did not burn.
I stood by the bonefire.
A raven and eagle wing quivered beside her.
Fire licks, jumps, leaps, throws itself
around them.
Two Old Ones observe, beckon me to come.
They smudge me with a white eagle feather.
Fire smothers the wings. The Old Ones
lift the wings, present them to me.
The wings shake and whisper,

> *She has a strong back. Much movement. She needs
> big wings.*

They attach themselves to my wound.

PROPHECY

I planted potatoes, zucchini, carrots, cabbage,
lettuce and peas, consumed them as they matured,
boiled, mashed in butter. Picked apples, plums,
nectarines, pears, berries. Scratched for nuts,
rosehips, currants. Canned, froze, layered them
into my hips with cheese, cream-soaked bread.
Breasts swayed, filled with gravy, stir-fry
venison, deep-fried mushrooms, ducks in
oatmeal soup, roasted beaver tail, bannock,
corn on the cob. I offered to my Beloved. His green-
Heavens slithered, stopped at my mounds.

> *Neanderthals gathered lard around their bellies,*

he informed me.
He lied when he said he'd love all my forms.
A deer kissed me, bear lay against my belly.
Buffalo charged, trampled him –
he became their groom.

> *I am getting old. I don't want to get old,*

he whined.
I lifted my gown,

> *Help yourself,*

I said. He humped. Filled his need.
Turned his back, went cold.

I remembered what the priest
said of us, and showed him:

"...when she divested herself of her clothing, and exposed herself to the air at the foot of a large cross that stands beside our cemetery. She did so at a time when snow was falling, although she was pregnant; and the snow that fell upon her back caused her so much suffering that she nearly died from it – as well as her child, when the cold chilled its mother's womb. It was her own idea to do this – to do penance for her sins, she said.

Two of them made a hole in the ice, in the depth of winter and threw themselves into the water, where they remained during the time it would take to say a rosary slowly and sedately." [3]

TOTEMS

I heard his lingered whisper:

>*I don't know what to do. I need to be told. I want to hold you.*
>*Am too afraid of the flood. I am weak. I am a forest in flames.*

I received a grail. A token. His totem.
Carved initials in a tree, graffiti on our garage door,
chalk figures on the sidewalk. Ochre rock paintings.
Crayon words. Old photographs. Mouse-torn letters.
Postcards. A juniper berry taped on paper. A song
of Burgundy wine. Inscriptions in a holy book.
Scorched, calligraphy pages;

>*I know I've been "away" for quite a while –*
>*and I'll remain "away" for quite a while later. Because*
>*I want to send you something "of me" to honour all the energy*
>*and friendship you've given over the years... Because I cannot*
>*give to you in any other way, I'm giving you this small collection*
>*I have saved for years. I could not think of anyone I could leave*
>*the collection with.*

I shook the manila that was stuffed between the
screen doors. Mouse turds, safety pins. Kidney bottle,
bobby pins, his drunk fingers scrawled:

>*I sure wish I was up there picking strawberries with you. I put*
>*a tough night last night. I lay awake most of the night. If I could*
>*quit thinking about you honey it might be a lot better for my*
>*health. I just got to see you pretty soon or I'll go nuts. My brother*
>*said the old broad was a wild moose at the dance the way she*
>*carried on. So Big Tits left her old man and went off to Alberta.*
>*Good for her. Everybody's leaving everyone nowadays. Same*
>*thing here. Boy, nobody stick out a lifetime. It's too damn long*
>*at a time to spend with one woman. Be careful of fire. Don't give*
>*up hopes. I skinny as a flatten frog, but I'll sees you soon.*

Snot ran in my laughter.

A DIFFICULT HOLY STRUGGLE

I don't touch him.

You called,

he stated.
I've barricaded Rib Woman so many times.
Repeatedly she sends an exam.
I am a failure.

> *You've given me a lopsided heart. Jagged and streaked. A*
> *weight in my pocket. I yearn to skim it in water.*
> *I've chosen to leave. I must live.*

He left his fingerprint on my thigh.

The lagoon is sluggish. I will drown.
I look for a way out.

> *Your calmness is everyone's excitement. A sweet pain*
> *I hide in thick books,*

he stated.

The Old One annointed my head,
feet, with bear grease. She dresses
me in yarns of night cloth.

The tell-dark is mine. A hole entered
where fingers fumble. Owls
scratch the doom. I placed a
pinch of tobacco. Still the dark
pries for the other side.

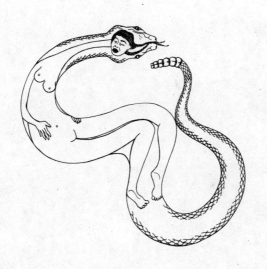

ALL IS REAL

Beloved and I digest
Rib Woman's, Rolling Head's
revelations. Driving the back roads'
clustered coppers, dimes, gold rings falling.

Stories are not told in spring, summer,
autumn. Too many listening Spirits
(though I know Spirits listen all the time.)
I'm too busy gardening, planting flowers,
picking berries, canning. I don't have
time to tell you a story. To have you listen.
When the geese drop snow feathers,
the restless spirits will no longer punish us.
Under this blanket some spirits will sleep,
others will watch the roll of language.
They will be swift with the winds
if I offend them.

Beloved and I follow a
SaskTel truck, it hits a spruce grouse.
I pluck feathers out of the window,
make our own SaskTel commercial.

We deliver the grouse to *aspin*.

MANYBERRIES

I followed the deer,
gave her fleshy oranges, apple cores.
She licked her fingers clean,
placed her wet nose on my Beloved.

> *We are coming. Coming.*

She lifted Beloved over logs, avoided swamps,
murky waters where snakes waited.

The deer arrived again, looked at me.
I carried Beloved, kissed the deer.
My knees buckled, deer's ears alert.
I lifted my pipe,
she kissed it tenderly. Repeatedly.
She smelled of sweet apples, orange juice.
Sat on her haunches, lifted her forearms,
hoofs cradled the pipe. *ospwâkan*
opened its eyes, lifted us into its lair.
The stone lit up and we entered a steep hill,
travelled through thorn trees, a bare windy path.
We moved into the swell, met our *wâhkômâkanak*.
One carried a cup and sang, voice musky,

> *The forked tongue of a river can never be separated. It*
> *shall always run deep,*

and poured rain.
Another relative decorated herself in starfish,
another was covered in pine pitch, wounds bandaged.
The moon exposed her many faces.
I was given a map, covered in Braille.
Leeches muscled out of aquariums,
Loch Ness toward the lakes.

A skunk waddled, sprayed us with medicine.
Mud-stained faces carried stick bundles,
built an island that drowned them.

Earth commanded Beloved to

Kiss me, kiss me. I ain't too vain to take these dentures out.

Rubbed against him

She doesn't have you, doesn't have you. I have you.

she sang, threw her arms around Beloved.
I stretched, full length
against his sinew. Earth sang,

We must chant our last song before the wind dies,

united all our breathing, covered us in
her quilted star blanket.
We wed again and again.

My Tribe

Everyone in boarding school was named after a saint.
Mary Wash Your Feet, Simple Simon, Peter Thumper.
My sister, Three Person was born again,
tore off her sweet love. The storm died,
he entered the skeleton hills. No more
White – Brown lovers. Men, they were all alike.

She tells me she'll have a duck dance.
Eyes closed she'll wring their necks, burn their scrolls,
release their buffalo, elk, deer, open net-caged fish.
The flesh-eaters will return amputated limbs. Sweet
kidneys will flush clear piss. No more candy apples,
cotton clouds, toffee, jelly bean, pistachio ice cream,
almond bars, chips, Pepsi, Big Mac, gravy, onion rings,
white bread. Weight Watchers would go broke. Fitness
centres would be empty. She knows this is my world.
Like me she wants the messengers, marathon runners,
the walkers to return. Bold warriors.
She carried *nôhkom*'s sausage, walked on *nôhkom*'s bologna
legs stuffed with Jesus and *pâhkahkos*.

       It was so tiring,

she said.

       Her grade two teacher gave her
       a shopping bag of high heels –
       in June she carried them on the bus home.
       At home she wrapped her pig in a banket,
       Pinky oinked her to sleep. Pinky, and her dogs
       Chico, Pick-up, ate bannock, leftover sandwiches.
       She rode Pinky, clung to his ears, oinked
       all over the yard. He died with his legs up.

       A big fat pig he became lard, and Indian popcorn.

       She laughed and laughed.

Round-dance

The young jazzed the round-dance,
answered the drum. Shuffled feet,
studied the floor. *aspin*, Gone-For-Good,
walked the circle shaking hands, hard of hearing.
People holler. She shrugs, turns down her lip,
laughs as if she's heard a good joke.
A middle-aged woman explains their
kinship. Gone-For-Good says loudly

> *I don't recognize you. You are all so fat.*

Followers cover their mouths.
Mother lectures –

> wâhkôhtowin *was a mess. Men donated bastards,*
> *left their seeds homeless, penniless. Father's Day is a mess.*

She forgot her one shoe, two shoe,
five shoe.

> *The Old people paid the hunters for rabbits, ducks, deer, fish.*
> *It was never like this.*

Silence filled the hall.
She was the last generation
and was allowed to speak
like this.
Another time I drove her to *manawânis* –
she saw a local drunk, rolled down her window
and yelled,

> *You good for nothin' son of a bit its. Go trapping.*

He gave her the thumbs up.

Your uncles say we don't come from animals – they've
forgotten wîsahkêcâhk, *his shifty ways. Wolf boy –* mahihkan.
They don't know nothin'. Pretend they have mamâhtâwisiwin *–*
special powers.

That night our relatives fill her.
Tomorrow when all is still, hands on hips,
in front of the picture window,
she'll watch the drive-away.
She will call Three Person, *wâpan,*
Mechanic or me, *ê-kwêskît –*

> *I thought one of yous was suffering. I didn't sleep all night.*
> *I told Onion Man one of yous was suffering. Gave him a prayer*
> *cloth.*

Bottom Feeder

I watched my mother, *aspin*,
watching Three Person, *wâpan* and me
disappear.
Down the hallway a large muskrat
lumbered toward her.
It leaped, its razor teeth clamped
her throat. She struggled.
A gray nun smiled crookedly as she
ushered her out.
aspin shared,

> *The night before my mother called. I followed her room to*
> *room. When I caught up I found a dog, curled like a*
> *newborn. Fur removed, stomach exposed, quivering though*
> *not in pain. It was as if it had an operation. I called Onion*
> *Man to help me kill it. He handed me a Winchester. I*
> *cocked and aimed. The barrel, it fell. I cocked, aimed*
> *again. The dog lifted its head, became your brother, my son,*
> *and asked me "Are you going to kill me, Mother?"*

Mother was hospitalized.

> *I couldn't reach my medicines. The buffalo put her head*
> *down. I stepped on it. I shall never eat her again. My belly*
> *was on fire, flames up my throat. Doctors couldn't find*
> *anything. I peed blood, shit covered in blood. I suffer now*
> *because* wâpistikwân, kôhkomak *beat me all my life.*

All night, she bled. A two-headed female moose,
puffed as oven-bread, staggered toward her.
It carried a baseball bat, lifted mother's
hospital gown shoved it up her bum.
Another elderly moose arrived, whispered,

You're a loose woman, have been all your life. We will
staple your spoon, make it look like perogy and send you
to a medicine man to remove your stitches.

Mother fell into a fevered sleep.
Sin, to her was an egg, a membrane
that pulsed, waiting for lightning to
crack its shell. Once cracked,
the sinner entered the other shore.
Mother asked me to let her off...remember
at the beginning we were bouncing
on an old rutted road
and I wanted her to
gather her bundles?
I watched her walk the hills –
she turned, waved and was swallowed.

Down South

I listened to Three Person, the White Goddess's rant.

> *I need a wire to barricade my heart, just like the concentration*
> *camps. I read about romantic fever in True Confessions.*
> *Lying Buggers. Cheating hearts all over the place.*
> *I made lots of soup to repair my bald spot, to heal my ripped*
> *Woman's. To heal this scarred one. Heart will learn these.*
> *I won't allow that woman aspin to coil around me like she's done*
> *already, to Onion Man.*
>
> *An eagle woke me last night, sat on my chest, peered at me as if*
> *she was an eye specialist. She helped me slather the bear grease.*
> *Her talons tattooed a monarch on my mound.*

THE LAST MESSAGE

That last spring when I stripped the lodge,
left it naked for the night with fresh willow
piled, the old lodge woke me.
The ribs of men, women, children struggled
to lift the ribbons, cloth, blankets they
had worn.
They sobbed as they worked.

Dear Magpie

Your frog that holds its legs against its body
wishes to return. For two weeks its insistence sat
on the tip of my ear. It started after
I found many of my own.

I have one, whose left leg curls into its belly,
the other leg still pushing forward.
I don't know what killed him.
There, safe on the hot road. No wheels to squish him.
I've seen others, headless, so still in movement, rushing
out of the way. Perhaps, it was exhaustion,
far from the slough, miles of hopping for a frog
though for us it is five hundred footprints.

I hope you are well. The frog tells me you are so,
though age eventually catches us,
mirrors our tired lines. Our youthful spirits
naughty and reflective lie to our bodies.
At least this is what I feel and see.

I hope you are well. Your book shares the story
I absorbed in the garden of your journey.
The spilled spirits who haunted your living
dissipated as your charge took life
and hugged it to your soul.

These days, ancient legends work their way
into how I've tasted, ate and swallowed my life.
I reframe them, hope they will live another way.
The wise live in the lake, sway in the tall grass,
light up the universe in the prairie storm.
I listen,
and eventually
the voices penetrate my thick skull

where my heart attempts
to understand.

These little frogs. Big ones too.
One sat in the folds of blankets –
its large eyes blocked our entrance
to Rib Woman.
Why would it choose to wrap itself
at the door in this prairie sweltering?

Then I remember
the large bullfrog
at the Old Indian Man's lodge.
It would hop in
when the flaps where open
and hop out when the sweat began.

Sweet wet babies, brown, green,
I hold them, release them into the slough.
These two, the one who yearns to return to you.
It just wants to go home.
And this one whose jump to heaven
in mid-death
it teaches me.

Walking Away

Have I told you his name?
It's been such a long journey.
We are almost finished.
Our time was filled with
breast-firm apples
that wept when our teeth crunched
into their white, white flesh.
Our bodies bent into each other
as we watched a blues singer
carry the mountains –

"All hearts will kill the assholes,"

she sang.

Later I watched Beloved
in conversation with him.
Beloved left him
standing.
Two trains approached one another.
I called into the hollowness.
The trains collided,
my love was thrown.
I crawled into his lair,
lifted his heart,
cradled it to my face.
There it beat.
So slow. So slow.

GAVE MY NAME

In the beginning

when these words were born

I, *ê-kwêskît*, Turn-Around Woman,

the sturgeon of the depths

swam since the day I drowned.

I never sleep.

When *ê-kwêskît* sinks,

head on pillow,

I surface

with camera, telephone, television

and a big screen.

âtayôhkan

For centuries

I've tumbled through thistles,

charcoal stars and sun,

groaning lakes and rivers,

my hairy skull

a home for mice and snakes.

A cursed man

chopped up my body,

sent my sons running. Now he swims

in stars,

nitêh my heart,
bleeding,
clutched in his fist.

I'm earth
born each moon,
waxing and waning,
bleeding eggs.
I'm painted red on rocks;
I swim the caves in lakes
where my head sinks.
And I drink to roll again.

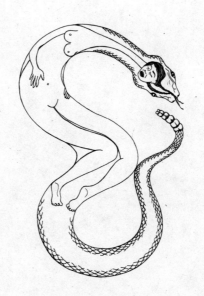

FOOTNOTES

1. Du Person, Father Francis. From *The Jesuit Relations and Allied Documents: A Selection Edited by S.R. Mealing*, The Carleton Library, #7; Toronto: McClelland & Stewart, 1963; Pages 55–56.

2. O'Meara, Walter. *Daughters of the Country: The Women of the Fur Traders and Mountain Men*. New York: Harcourt, Brace & World, Inc, 1968; Page 105.

3. Mealing, S.R., ed. *The Jesuit Relations and Allied Documents: A Selection Edited by S.R. Mealing*, The Carleton Library, #7; Toronto: McClelland & Stewart, 1963; Page 88.

GLOSSARY

aspin, Gone-For-Good; used as a
personal name

awâsis, child

âpihtâ-kîsikânohk, towards the half
day, noon, south

âpihtâ-kîsikâw, It is noon. It is half
day

âstam, come (sg)

âstamik, come (pl)

âstamik. pê-kîwêk, come (pl) come
home (pl)

âtayôhkan, spirit being; spiritual
entity; ancient legend spirit (sg)

âtayôhkanak, spirit beings; spiritual
entities; ancient legend spirits (pl)

âtayôhkêwin, a sacred story

cihcipistikwân, Rolling Head

cihcipistikwân-âtayôhkêwin, Sacred
story of the Rolling Head

cîpayak, ghosts (pl)

ê-kî-mamâhtâwisicik iyiniwak,
People were gifted with Mystery

ê-kwêskît, 1.S/he turns around;
2. personal name given to a
female: Turn-Around Woman

êkwa, and

êsa, I understand; apparently

iyiniwak, First Nations people,
Indians

kayâs, long ago

kayâs ê-kî-mamâhtâwisicik iyiniwak,
a long time ago people were filled
the gift of Mystery – spiritual gifts
that materialize in gifted people

kayâs êsa, ancient times; a long, long
time ago

kâ-kitocik, Thunder Beings. They
who thunder

kêhtê-aya, an elderly person

kêhtê-iyiniw, an old man

kiskânak, bitch

kî-mamâhtâwisiwak, They were
spiritually gifted people

kîwêk, go home (pl)

kîwêtinohk, north, in the north,
towards the north wind, home, to
carry home

kîwêtinotâhk, north, in the north,
towards the north wind

kôhkom, your grandmother (sg)

kôhkomak, your grandmothers (pl)

kôkom, Grandma! (vocative or
address form)

maci-manitow, the devil (more
specifically a devil-god)

mahihkan, wolf

mamâhtâwêyihtâkosiwin, special
powers, gifted spiritually; usually
in referring to a medicine person
with shamanistic abilities

mamâhtâwisiwak, They have supernatural power; They are gifted spiritually

manawânis, a town; a place where one collects extra goods, ie. food/clothing/tools. This word has other implications.

mâmaskâc, amazing

mâtahikan, a tool used for fleshing/scraping fur off of an animal skin

miskîsikwa, 1. eyes; 2. One's Big Heavens

mitêwiwin, Midewin Society, Medicine Society

mosom, Grandpa! (vocative or address form)

nêhiyaw, a Cree person

nêhiyânâhk, in Cree country

nika-kisyâkin, I'd tell a lie

nikosis, my son

nikosisak, my sons (pl)

nimosôm, my grandfather

nipêpîm, my baby

nipêpîmak, my babies (pl)

nisto-iyiniw, Three-Person

nitêh, my heart

nôhkom, my grandmother

nôhkomak, my grandmothers (pl)

nôhkomis, my little grandma (an

endearment), "my uncle" in some communities where the Cree "n" dialect is spoken

nôtokwêsiw, an old woman

okiskêyihtamowin, 1. his/her knowledge, experience; 2. knowing

ospwâkan, 1. pipe (for smoking); 2. used as a personal name, Pipe

pâhkahkos, 1. Bony Spectre, Hunger spirit, spirit being 2. flying skeleton

pâhpiwiyiniw, 1. literally: The man is laughing; 2. used as a personal name, Laughing Man

pahkisimotâhk, 1. west, in the west, towards the sunset; 2. where the sun falls, a falling away

pimîhkân, pemmican

pisikwâtisak, 1. those who are bold with opposite sex or commit adultery; 2. loose sexually

sâkahikan, lake

sâkâstênohk, towards the sunrise, east, in the east; rising sun

sâkâstêw, sunrise

sîpiy, river

tawinikêwin, spacious beautiful, abundance of land; a cleared space; spacious creation

wâhkômâkanak, relatives, kin; the crooked relatives, or, more specifically, walking in a bent-over way among the relatives

wâpan, 1. It is dawn, morning; 2.
used as a personal name,
Morning or Dawn

wâpanotâhk, towards the sunrise,
east, in the east

wâpistikwân, 1. white hair; 2. used as
a personal name, White Hair

wêpinâson, 1. ceremonial cloth, cloth
offering; 2. prayer cloth, an
offering. Without being
disrespectful, the closest
translation is an offering, in
particular, a cloth that is being
thrown away but in gesture of a
give-away or offering more than
the actual casting away. Perhaps
more specifically, a sacred
offering/throw away which flies
in the wind.

wiyin, fat

wiyipiyiniw, Filthy Man; used as a
personal name in this story

wîhcêki-sâkahikan, a stinky lake;
Stinking Lake

wîhkês, 1. muskrat root, rat root,
sweet flag, water arum; 2. a bitter
root that is used as a medicine for
colds and other ailments

wîhtikow, 1. *Wihtikow, Windigo;*
cannibal, giant man-eating
monster; 2. cannibalistic creature.
Not spoken about because of its
intense power – especially during
winter – or else famine will strike.

wîhtikow sâkahikan, Cannibal Lake;
a fictitious name, a fabricated
location

wîsahkêcâhk, 1. Cree culture hero,
legendary figure; 2. Cree trickster
whose antics teach lessons; 3. a
bitter Cree

IN APPRECIATION WITH GRATITUDE

To the Great Mystery
I thank you for the wind that gives me breath and direction.
To the water that keeps me afloat, bathes and quenches my thirst.
The sun that gives warmth, nourishes my food and enlightens my
    thoughts.
To the earth, her beauty and her abundance and all that she offers.
All my relations.

The Crooked Good has been an on-going project for many years. It
went through many transitions. A number of the poems in this
collection have previously appeared, sometimes in slightly different
forms, in the periodical *The Structurist,* and others, in *The March
Hare* anthology and on CBC Radio.

I am grateful to the Saskatchewan Arts Board for their initial
funding.

Paul Fleck's Scholarship provided by the Banff Centre for the Arts
kept me in the various bush studios. Thank you for rooms, food and
Mr. Fleck's generous gift.

Emma Lake Kenderline Campus gave me lodgings and a studio in
support of the Saskatchewan Writer's Guild's Poet Laureate program.
For a full week I walked among their pines, and this project
continued its long labour. Thank you.

Coteau for being so patient and giving *The Crooked Good* its final
form and birth.

I miss both my finest mentors, the late Dr. David S. Barnes and J. P
Cardinal. They continue to be my constant companions.

Louise Million and Vera Martin, I remember our travels, thank you
for your generous teachings.

Peter, thank you for your wisdom, patience, and being such a respectful, challenging partner and teacher. I couldn't ask for a finer friend and husband. I owe you this.

Seán Virgo for your wicked eye, your laughter, your wisdom, active curiosity, and your incredible editorial talent. I am so very grateful and enriched.

Jean Okimâsis for your careful work on the Cree language, and for your enthusiasm.

Paul LaPointe your friendship and your art is our blessing.

Thank you to our elder and friend Marie Linklater for her laughter, wisdom and story-sharing.

Omeasoo, my daughter, I am so privileged to have shared with you Rib Woman and her Mystery in the Saddle Lake hills and our Cardinal family. I am so proud of you.

Usne, Trisha and the boys, Alistair Aski and Josiah Kesic. Because you're enthralled by "The Rolling Head" I pass this unto you.

Mother, I thank you for being the Legend Keeper and passing it on in the first place.

Martha Half for the care you've given mother, your kindness, your struggles, and for the sharing of your journey.

Nancy Waskewitch for keeping the legend alive.

Ron and Patti Marken for the many years of friendship and loyalty: you've given us such a gift.

Jane Urquhart for your exuberance and "knowing in your heart," I delight in this.

Tim Lilburn for your encouragement and our shared walk.

Paulette Dube for lending me your ears and the many years of laughter.

Jan Salkerd for reading the original thought.

Keith Manley for sharing the parch with Omeasoo, Peter and me.

Rosemary Nixon for the exploration, laughter and wisdom.

Rupert Ross for your valuable insights, may they too travel in the winds.

To all of my other family, the fasters, the friends, the lodge. Your support is profound. An extended apology for those unmentioned – so many people, so many stories – thank you. I mean no harm, only good blessings.

This story couldn't be told without love and strife as dual companions. So many people are enriched and hurt by the expression and misunderstanding of love. Love is a trickster. I hope, however, that in this walk wisdom is gained.

I have dreamt, been given and collected many stories over the years. The themes are all too common but their expressions so varied. I offer this story as a way to go inward, so that one may go forward perhaps a little more intact. That is all.

Megweetch to all of you for your generosity. All my relations.

AUTHOR PHOTO: KASDORF STUDIOS

ABOUT THE AUTHOR

Louise Bernice Halfe has two previous book publications to her credit: *Bear Bones & Feathers* published in 1994, received the Canadian Peoples Poet Award, and was a finalist for the Spirit of Saskatchewan Award that year. *Blue Marrow,* released in its revised edition by Coteau Books in 2004, was a finalist for both the Governor General's Award for Poetry and the Pat Lowther Award, and for the 1998 Saskatchewan Poetry and Saskatchewan Book of the Year awards.

Louise made her debut as a poet in *Writing the Circle: Native Women of Western Canada,* the acclaimed anthology of life-writings by Native women. She was awarded third prize in the League of Canadian Poets' national poetry contest in 1993, and was Saskatchewan's Poet Laureate in 2005 and 2006.

Louise Bernice Halfe's Cree name is Sky Dancer. She was born on the Saddle Lake Reserve in Two Hills, Alberta in 1953. She currently lives near Saskatoon with her husband.